Thanks to Her

Thanks to Her

FINDING POWER AND INSPIRATION IN YOUR FAMILY PHOTOS

by Kathleen Geraghty

Copyright © 2020 by Kathleen Geraghty.

ISBN 978-1-7349295-0-8

All rights reserved. No part of this document may be reproduced or transmitted in any form or by any means, electronic, mechanical, photocopying, recording, or otherwise, without prior written permission of the publisher.

Library of Congress Control Number: 2020908678

Cover design by Maraldi Design, Chicago.

This book is dedicated to every female whose photograph appears on its pages.

Hello, It's Me!
My name is Kathleen Geraghty. I am a former newspaper photojournalist who loves pictures and appreciates a good story. In my spare time, I enjoy talking to strangers and asking their opinions on any number of matters. People are hilarious!

Once Upon a Time:
In my childhood, I was known to play topless baseball in Riis Park.

Author's Note:

In writing this book, I spent countless hours dwelling in the photographic past. Specifically, I examined what American women accomplished (or at the very least, had to tolerate) between 1900 and 1950. These were action-packed decades in our country's history and it's no exaggeration to say that females did much of the heavy lifting during them.

Even more impressive were the various changes our foremothers managed to effect. They never quit, even though they were discouraged at virtually every turn by a patriarchal society that told them to stay home, mind the children, look pretty, and remain silent. I am inspired by what these women did to improve our world. It's my hope that a "Thanks to Her" photo project will leave you feeling estrogen-fueled and ready to rumble as well.

I acknowledge that my editorial approach subtly reflects my own upbringing and personal experiences. I am an American girl from the Northwest Side of Chicago. I was, like so many of my pre-Internet contemporaries, raised on promises, fashion magazines, O-Ke-Doke Cheese Popcorn, and lots and lots of mind-bending TV.

"Thanks to Her" was created for any female who has been told they "can't" or "won't" or "will never" — and that their dreams and goals are unattainable. I beg to differ. For you, I offer these words of wisdom from one of my more colorful college roommates, Barb "Barbeque" Pakieser, who said this in regard to life's challenges, its setbacks, and starting anew:

"That movie is over. Some parts of it were OK, but it really wasn't that great. It's time to throw away your popcorn, leave the dark theater and head out into the sunlight. It might hurt your eyes in the beginning, but it will be worth it in the long run."

Table of Contents

Introduction: Who's That Girl? The Story of Hazel 11

Chapter One: Yes, She Did and So Can You 15

Chapter Two: I'm So Exhausted and Cranky! Why Do This at All? 21

Chapter Three: What's the Deal with Photos, Anyway? 27

Chapter Four: Where Did We Put That Old Shoebox? 33

Chapter Five: The Cost of Photography: Lookin' Good (If We Can Afford It) 49

Chapter Six: Home, Heart, Head 59

Chapter Seven: Let's Take It One Decade at a Time 64
- 1900s: New Ideas, New Technologies and The New Woman 68
- 1910s: World War I, Social Protests and The Spanish Influenza 84
- 1920s: Flappers, Speakeasies, Bathtub Gin and Jazz 104
- 1930s: The Great Depression, Dust Storms and The New Deal 126
- 1940s: World War II, Rations and Rosie the Riveter 150

Chapter Eight: Spotlight on Technology: An Ode to the Washing Machine 168

Chapter Nine: C'mon Over, It's Party Time! 174

Chapter Ten: Considering the "Big Picture" 184

Chapter Eleven: Now, It's Your Turn! 196
- Women's History Resources 200
- Thanks to Them 203

For most of history, Anonymous

was a *woman*.

Who's That Girl?
The Story of Hazel

"Take care of your inner, spiritual beauty. That will reflect in your face."

—Dolores del Rio (1904-1983), first major female Latin-American movie star
to have crossover appeal in Hollywood

Make no mistake: I love a garage sale. You never know what you're going to find. Could be a set of amber-colored milk bottles from a now-defunct dairy. Could be a vintage birdbath that needs a coat of paint and a little TLC. Could be a wooden crate that was used to ship a bomb fuse to Chicago in the 1940s. (Yes. I have actually found and gleefully purchased all these things.)

My hoarder tendencies were on red alert one day in May of 2016 as I strolled up a suburban driveway to pick through someone else's tchotchkes. The fact that we were getting ready to sell our house and I was in the process of donating and/or packing up all my earthly treasures did not stop me from coveting a few more.

The homeowners were nice people, chatting it up with the dozen or so shoppers who were already on site. The man of the house was sorting dusty tools and hardware on a table next to me when I saw the photo for the first time. It was sticking up out of cracked shoebox, propped up rather haphazardly against some funky, filthy old Christmas garland.

It was a sepia-colored print that looked like the cardboard had been trimmed by hand. The edges were worn, but the image itself was in pretty good condition. The photograph showed a young woman with wavy hair who gazed at the camera with the tiniest bit of a Mona Lisa smile. Her eyes were gorgeous. I flipped the photo over and saw spidery handwriting on the back. It read: "Hazel. About 20 years old."

"Did you mean to sell this photo?" I asked the man. "Who's Hazel?" He squinted and peered across the table in the bright sunlight. "Oh, I have no idea who that is," he said. "I'm not even sure where that picture came from. I found it in a box in the basement."

I told him that I was a photographer and that I thought it was a beautiful image. "You like it?" he said. "Why don't you take it? I'll let you have it for nothing."

It was unsettling for me to learn that such a nice portrait could have no value ... and that its origin was a mystery. This woman had obviously been important to someone, somewhere, during her lifetime.

After a brief discussion, I wound up making a cash donation to the garage sale and I took Hazel home with me. I didn't know what I was going to do with her — I have thousands of old prints, negatives, slides and photo CDs of my own creation that take up vast amounts of storage space in my house. My office runneth over.

But, I really liked her face and I decided that she deserved better. Hazel stayed in a bin on my desk for more than a year. Every so often, I would pick up the photo and study her hairstyle, her clothing and her beautiful eyes. I wondered what she had been thinking when the photographer made her portrait. What was her life all about?

Eventually, my curiosity got the better of me. I shared Hazel's portrait with a handful of people, asking for their opinions on its provenance. A vintage fashion expert I consulted was able to date the image to the 1920s. She said that it appears as though, in an effort to approximate the very daring "bobbed" hairstyles of the day, Hazel pulled her long hair back into a loose bun. She also said that Hazel's dress looks to be made of white cotton voile and is accented with French corded trim — an embellishment that suggests she might have been a person of some financial means.

To this day, I don't know exactly who Hazel was, where she lived or what became of her. However, I am still certain that she deserves to be remembered. All the more reason for her to be on the cover of this book.

There are millions of Hazels out there. You know their stories. I hope this particular anonymous young woman inspires you to share your family photos and the stories behind them while the precious details are still easily accessible. They might be the key to a better future for us all.

Above:
Back side of Hazel's portrait, 1920s.

Opposite Page:
Woman's personal items, jewelry and house key, circa 1920s.
Photograph by Kathleen Geraghty.

Previous Spread:
Left: Studio portait of Hazel, an unknown young woman, 1920s.

Right: Snapshot. Two anonymous women waving at the camera. Date and location unknown.

Chapter 1:
Yes, She Did and So Can You.

"God may be in the details, but the goddess is in the questions. Once we begin to ask them, there's no turning back."

— Gloria Steinem (1934-), American feminist, journalist, editor and equal rights activist

Hello, Ladies. Good morning. Good evening. Happy New Year! Happy Birthday! Shalom. Namaste. Pick the salutation that works for you, depending on the time and date you have chosen to open this book, and your overall spiritual vibe. I would also like to add: Congratulations! You are on a Heroine's Journey. Did you know that? Well, it's true, God love ya!

Every morning, when you spring out of bed (immaculately coiffed and in full makeup, wearing a lace teddy and red Manolos, just like me) you are embarking on the adventure that is your life. You are facing the unknown. Absolutely anything can happen — and most days, it does.

It doesn't matter what kind of 24-hour experience you're having. Perhaps it's a blissful, pineapple-infused vacation day in the tropics. Or maybe it's a full-tilt urban meltdown, a day when your car breaks down on the highway and your cell phone is at home on the kitchen table. It could even be a special occasion like your high school graduation, or your long-awaited release from federal prison, or the first time you win the Oscar for Best Actress. Yay! It's all good!

The very fact that today you woke up and faced life meant that you were heading out on a new Heroine's Journey. In mythological terms, this type of adventure represents a distinct period of time in which you (The Heroine) tackle challenges, meet mentors, fight off dangers, and emerge victorious — before returning home transformed and so very much wiser.

Every day, you encounter situations that might fall anywhere on the spectrum from glorious to craptacular. No matter what, as a Fabulous Modern Woman, you fire up your brain, determine a course of action and proceed.

For example, today's adventure could be as small as eating cookies right out of the bag while shopping at Costco. It could be as large as boarding a private jet for a business lunch in Milan. When it's over and you lay your head on your favorite pillow at night, you've completed one specific 24-hour Heroine's Journey.

Previous Spread, Left:
Top Left: Portrait, Native American woman wearing traditional clothing, late 1910s.

Top Right: Snapshot, women in summer dresses, late 1920s or early 1930s.

Bottom Left: Snapshot, women wearing men's suits and hats (specifically, left to right: a fedora, a bowler, and a cap), 1930s.

Bottom Right: Snapshot, woman in cuffed jeans posing near highway sign, late 1940s or early 1950s.

Previous Spread, Right:
Snapshot, pensive woman sitting on top of Easter Rock, 1910s.

This Page:
Snapshot, female crew members dressed in work clothes and hard hats, late 1930s or early 1940s.

In times of social upheaval, the two World Wars included, American women were allowed to step into lucrative jobs that were traditionally held by male workers. While the wages were higher than what they might have earned doing "women's work," female employees were paid less for doing the same jobs, and dismissed when the number of available male workers returned to normal levels.

Then, you rise and shine in the morning, ready for the next day's adventure. And the next. And the next. This cycle continues every week, every month, every year — and eventually becomes the more complex Heroine's Journey that is your Life, with a capital L.

In each instance, in any adventure you launch, you are following the lead of our female ancestors, tracing their steps and building on their knowledge. Thanks to their various efforts and achievements, these women serve as our spiritual guides. They're kind of like an all-seeing and ever-present Magic 8-Ball, helping us find the answers we need. Which brings me to my point, and I do have one ...

Why is "Thanks to Her" the book for you?

As Fabulous Modern Women, our daily schedules are jam-packed and our responsibilities are many. When we do finally carve out a chunk of time to devote to R&R and reading, the options floating around in the free marketplace of ideas are so voluminous, it's almost impossible to focus. As a matter of fact, my eyes are already crossing as I type this ...

Should you allocate an hour to a self-improvement book? Catch up on world news and politics? Flip through that financial planning guide? These are all practical and worthwhile pursuits, but in the interest of decompressing, doesn't that tawdry mystery novel have more allure?

Actually, if we want to get real on the subject of leisure, how is a woman supposed to pencil in time for reading and enrichment? There are barely enough hours in the day to obsess over our body fat and practice our self-loathing techniques. And of course, there's the looming certainty of yet another Heroine's Journey on tap for tomorrow ...

Out of the Studio and Into the World:
Travel and recreation photos became more common as the 20th century progressed and consumers became more comfortable with the medium of photography. These images are powerful visual keepsakes that document the Heroine's Journeys that were taken by the ladies who came before us.

Opposite Page:
Top Left: Art Deco-style snapshot, building and location unknown, 1930s.

Top Right: Snapshot, woman on a dock or pier, feeding a treat to a dog, late 1940s.

Bottom Left: Snapshot, view from plane's window taken mid-flight, 1940s.

Bottom Right: Snapshot, women on a nature hike, 1920s. This is perfect Heroine's Journey attire! Note sensible walking shoes, floppy sunhat and the "middy blouse," which was not tucked in and resembled a sailor's uniform. In the 1910s, the cotton middy included a belt, but by the 1920s, that feature had disappeared in favor of a wide band at the bottom hem. This new incarnation of the garment was loose and facilitated movement, making it suitable for gym, camp or sports.

Above:
Snapshot, well-dressed woman posing near porch steps in ginormous, fur-covered white hat, late 1900s. Shades of Yosemite Sam!

Below:
Woman in headscarf on laundry day. Photo mounted on cardstock. Date, location, original format unknown.

To quote the late, great Doris Day, Hollywood's quintessential 1950s uber virgin and put-upon career gal: "What's a girl to do?!" While reading this page, you might be thinking, *"Lordy, I didn't know there would be a test involved when I cracked this thing open! Quit grilling me!"*

Forgive me, my lady-buddy-friend. Kick back in your comfy clothes. Listen to some calming whale sounds on YouTube. Get into a tranquil head space. Then, slather on your favorite pore-shrinking face mask and let me bullet-point the highlights for you. Simply put:

- "Thanks to Her" will inspire you to locate, review and share your family photos. The images of your female relatives are, in essence, time capsules that can tell the story of what American women have been able to achieve, against all odds and in the face of adversity.
- "Thanks to Her" can start a dialogue between females of all ages and walks of life and help us honor our foremothers.
- "Thanks to Her" can be the emotional rocket fuel that will power all your future Heroine's Journeys, whether large or small.

"Thanks to Her" is the book for you if you are:

- Chillaxing in a teenage daydream
- Younger than springtime and still getting asked for your ID
- A raging ball of hormones (And thanks so much for asking!)
- Firm and fit and able to wear a bathing suit in public
- A pregnant woman (Don't even think of messing with me.)
- A mom or caregiver
- A girlfriend, spouse or partner
- A lover or a fighter
- A middle-aged woman (Living the dream, baby!)
- Mature, elegant and unique — like a fine wine
- Old enough to know better and embracing every wrinkle
- Sick and tired of being told what to do
- Ready to kick some ass
- Just getting done kicking some ass
- In the mood for a few laughs

"Thanks to Her" is the book that can help you:

- Tell your own story, preferably in a dramatic manner
- Spend a tranquil evening looking at old photos, while sipping cocktails and talking to yourself (ages 21+ only)
- Examine your past (Lifeline tracing is optional!)
- Analyze the multifaceted lives of the women who raised you

- Admire some extremely funky hairstyles and fashions
- Review your family history, for better or for worse, and compile a scholarly critique for your relatives to read. Consider a catchy title like "From Corsets to Girdles: A Retrospective" or "Who Could've Ever Seen *That* Coming?" or "This Explains a Lot About You."
- Clean out some old resentments, including the voodoo curses
- Enlighten (and possibly frighten) young women with homespun stories of the olden days
- Convince little girls that they can accomplish big, magical, fabulous things, especially when they are wearing tutus
- Gain a little perspective and a little wisdom
- Consider the mind-blowing arc of women's achievements in the first half of the 20th century

Still with me? Then read on, Lady Jane. Read on…

The Deckled Edge Snapshot:
Both the images on this page feature what is known as a "deckled edge." This method of trimming photographic prints was meant to imitate the appearance of fine art paper. The technique suggests that by the mid-20th century, photographs (even the ubiquitous snapshot) had gained recognition as a genuine visual art form.

This Page, Top:
Snapshot, woman seated on outdoor bench, dated on back "12-6-1944." (Note presence of the photographer's stalker-esque shadow in the foreground. Cool, huh?)

This Page, Bottom:
Snapshot, ultra-glam woman reclining on urban rooftop, 1950s.

Chapter 2:
I'm So Exhausted and Cranky! Why Do This at All?

"The most common way people give up their power is by thinking they don't have any."
— *Alice Walker (1944 -), American novelist, poet, activist and Pulitzer Prize winner*

Why should you start a "Thanks to Her" photo project — or anything, for that matter? Why not just continue to lump along, living a very beige life and wringing your hands about the state of affairs in this crazy world? Well, I'm not trying to be "The Boss of You," but I can make a recommendation.

First and foremost, by reviewing the past, we can honor the efforts of those ladies who toted the weary load so that conditions in our homes, our communities and our world might improve.

Secondly, when you open those dusty photo boxes and albums, you may find that you're discovering and uncovering some of the crapola that's holding you back in your own life. And once those doors are opened, the beliefs and attitudes that no longer benefit you can be discarded. (Consider it a cerebral spring cleaning or a psychic high colonic — you pick.)

I think that most of the females walking around on this planet manage to keep their rage simmering at a low boil. In America, we live with an underlying current of anger over what we see happening in our country, over how we are patronized, devalued and discriminated against as a gender.

Every time another story hits the news about a man in power pulling out his wee-wee and waving it at 20-year-old coed during her job interview, we want to barf. Depending on how detailed the media coverage is, some of us do.

Every time another wife goes "missing" and the cops start looking at her husband, who, coincidentally, has a history of domestic violence, we shake our heads in disgust. We wonder ... what would happen if some of these wife beaters started disappearing without a trace?

Every time our elected officials ignore the pressing needs of women and families (particularly those who are living in poverty), a little piece of our collective soul shrivels up and dies. It makes you think: What would be my fate if I hit the skids? Would I be

Previous Spread, Left:
Studio portrait of unknown woman, mid-20th century.

Previous Spread, Right:
Lee, Russell, photographer. Mexican woman in kitchen corner of her one-room dwelling made out of discarded tin ceiling material. Notice dirt floor. Robstown, Nueces County, Texas. United States. 1939. Feb. Photograph. https://www.loc.gov/item/2017782266/.

able to rely on the kindness of strangers? Or would I end up like Blanche DuBois, hauled off to a Louisiana insane asylum without even so much as a fare-thee-well?

We voice our disapproval, but it often feels like nobody is listening. It's like being a contestant on a rigged game show. Your buzzer doesn't work half the time and you can't weigh in with your answer, although you very well know the price of a washer-dryer combo, for cryin' out loud!

But, wait! There's more to this societal game show than what's visible to the naked eye! Take a look at what's behind Curtain Number Three! It's economic inequality! Ohhh, too bad, so sad! Yes, women have been sold the same rotten equal-pay bill of goods over and over and over again since June Cleaver was mopping the kitchen floor in her pearls, pencil skirt and demure, low-heeled pumps.

> The Equal Pay Act of 1963 made it illegal for employers to pay men more than women for doing the same job. Amazingly, more than 50 years later, we still have a gender wage gap.

Since our families are depending on us, women still keep trying to stretch our "pink collar" 80-cents-to-the-man's-dollar wages at the grocery store and the dreaded Walmart. We keep fighting the good fight.

Life in America in this day and age isn't exactly a Utopian dream. However, nothing good ever comes out of quitting. It's like Harriet Beecher Stowe said: "Never give up, for that is just the place and time that the tide will turn." Quite a bold message from a lady who's been dead for more than 100 years. Makes me want to put on a hoop skirt and a bonnet and tear up the town, with my Fitbit tallying every step along the way.

The fact is that women have been 50 percent responsible for the survival and the success of the human race. That's quite an accomplishment. Furthermore, when I was testing this book idea with focus groups of complete strangers I met at the pawn shop, the DMV and my favorite hair salon, I learned some amazing things. Right from the get-go, I discovered that many people are crabby. No surprise there. I also found that every single subject I forcibly interviewed had a story.

Some of these stories were frightening. Others involved criminal activity or light treason, which I considered fascinating. What was most intriguing was that every respondent was eager to share an anecdote about a female powerhouse in their own family. This was generally a woman who had faced daunting challenges in the interest of keeping those she loved clothed, fed and safe. I came away from these encounters with a powerful realization: Maybe a book could inspire women to use their amazing

female-centric family stories for the greater good. And imagine what might happen if women shared their vintage family photos along with all those remarkable stories!

I envisioned the sacred, ceremonial transfer of pearls of wisdom between the generations. Some of those pearls would be handed down with tender loving care, in gentle one-on-one discussions. Others would be lobbed into unfiltered conversations like live hand grenades, in the spirit of a revolution! Either way, this idea was sounding quite promising.

Today, we stand on the shoulders of the women who came before us. Tomorrow, future generations will stand on ours. What kind of legacy do we want to leave them? Can we best guide them by viewing our own troubles and conflicts with a "glass-half-full" mentality? Would it be beneficial to teach them that they can accomplish virtually anything when armed with creativity and determination — two priceless character traits? Our grandmothers might have had scant resources, but there's no doubt that they were nothing short of miracle workers. This is where a "Thanks to Her" photo project can be inspiring. Better still, it can serve as means of supercharging the power that all females have right here, right now.

This Spread:
Images from the Women's March on Chicago in 2017 and 2018. Photographs by Kathleen Geraghty.

There is a process called "Asset-Based Organizing" that is being put into use today in many urban areas. It suggests that social and economic revitalization begins with discovering and mobilizing the assets that are already present in every community. For example, that rundown Art Deco movie theater shouldn't be viewed as an eyesore to be razed to make way for a strip mall. It should be honored as an architectural jewel that's ready for its second act. With a bit of volunteerism, planning, and creative fundraising, that theater might be transformed into a mixed-use community center in which thousands of lives can be enriched. Everybody wins and the local history is preserved. The only downside to Asset-Based Organizing is that it requires that we get off our asses.

> From a theoretical standpoint, a "Thanks to Her" photo project can serve as a form of Asset-Based Organizing not only for our individual families, but for the next generation of women. What we, as females, have accomplished in the past has value. Our contributions deserve to be showcased and praised. Most importantly, we need to take stock of where we've been so that we might chart a course for the future.

Women can mobilize. Charity may begin at home, but so does activism. As individual women and families, we can summon the same resolute spirit that helped our foremothers succeed and use it to move America forward. Together, we can make a shift from a culture of dominance, run by patriarchal hierarchies, to a culture of partnership, based on mutual respect, intellectual and spiritual growth, and participatory democratic processes.

> And you thought this was just about looking at some old pictures ...

This Spread:
Images from the Women's March on Chicago in 2017 and 2018.
Photographs by Kathleen Geraghty.

sandra 6½

Chapter 3:
What's the Deal with Photos, Anyway?

"Photography takes an instant out of time, altering life by holding it still."

— *Dorothea Lange (1895-1965), American photojournalist who chronicled the Great Depression*

When I was 10 years old, the back porch sunroom in my parents' house was my favorite place to waste a summer afternoon. It was the perfect spot to curl up, read, and imagine what life would be like if I had been born into a different and much wealthier family.

In those prehistoric times, we only had six TV channels to choose from and midday programming consisted primarily of soap operas. Comic books and *MAD* magazine seemed more grounded in reality than the hijinks on "The Edge of Night," so that was where I focused my attention.

After devouring the fashion-infused adventures of Betty and Veronica at Riverdale High, I would flip back over the more dramatic illustrations and wonder if I would ever develop an hourglass figure and a set of melon-sized jugs like the ones those mini-skirted cartoon girls sported. Then, I would waste more time lingering over the issue's back pages, studying ads for must-haves like Amazing X-Ray Specs and packages of live Sea Monkeys. I vividly recall an ad that featured a black-and-white photo of a young man holding a 35mm camera. The headline read: "I can't draw, but photography made me an artist!" He wore a groovy, fringed vest and had a slouching, anti-establishment posture that willed me to believe him.

I did feel a twinge of jealousy deep down, because as a female, I had been led to believe there were three career options available to me: teacher, nurse or secretary. If, by some freakish turn of events, I exhibited an adventurous streak and a touch of wanderlust, I could take a bold leap into a new frontier and become an airline stewardess! *(I'm Kathy! Fly Me!)*

Yet, here was this shaggy guy, bragging that with a camera in his hands, he was gonna be the next Norman Rockwell. What piqued my interest most of all was the fact that this dude was admitting that he couldn't draw — not one bit. Now, I had been sweating over my drawing and painting skills since my first day of kindergarten. I liked art projects and could easily create a picture of my family standing in front of our

Previous Spread, Left:
Images of young girls in various socially acceptable roles of the early 20th century.

Top Left: Snapshot, future mother in the snow with baby doll, late 1910s.

Top Right: Snapshot, cheerleaders, 1936.

Bottom Left: Snapshot, aspiring nurses, late 1930s or early 1940s.

Bottom Right: Snapshot, girl in training to be a "Lady Who Lunches," late 1940s.

Previous Spread, Right:
Dorothea Lange, Resettlement Administration photographer, in California. United States, February, 1936. Photograph. https://www.loc.gov/item/2017759800/.

Below:
A visual representation of a sad chapter in a young girl's life: "The Funkified Toast Incident That Started It All."

house, with a big, yellow sun beaming overhead. Throw in a few tulips and I could whip up a fairly decent greeting card for just about any occasion.

But in fourth grade, when given the assignment in science class of drawing the components of a balanced breakfast, I drew a piece of toast that looked kinda lopsided. The more I tried to fix it, the worse it got, until what started out as my golden slice of buttered Wonder Bread more closely resembled a carcinogenic kidney bean.

My friend Chrissy — who was one of the best artists in our class — leaned across the aisle, studied my drawing and laughed out loud. She tapped the boy seated in front of her, pointed at my paper and said, "Hey, look at her bread! That's just a dirty piece of burnt toast!" He started snickering, too. That gave Chrissy all the encouragement she needed. *"Is that what your mother makes for breakfast?"* she asked in a giggling stage whisper. *"Do you put jelly on that?"*

I tried to defend myself to no avail. People were getting a real kick out of my crummy artwork. When the boy who sat on the other side of the aisle craned his neck and announced, "That looks like *poo*," Chrissy laughed so hard that drool trickled out of her mouth onto her own paper, which caused her to double over in a heap. "It's the *worst* piece of toast I've ever seen," she gasped, with her cheek mashed down on her desk and her shoulders shaking with laughter. (Always a bit avant-garde, Chrissy would later that day go on a paste-eating bender that would inspire our teacher, Mrs. Keane, to punish her by making her sit behind the industrial-sized garbage can in front of the classroom.)

While this mockery didn't stop me from loving art, it was the first brick in the proverbial wall. I was starting to see that maybe I didn't have what it took to be a real artist. I was a sham. A pretender. A wannabe bread-drawer. So, imagine my surprise when this Hipster Doofus in the back of a comic book presented me with a new possibility, another way to embrace creativity. Photography could make you an artist? Who knew?

Never one to give up or listen to reason, I spent the bulk of my high school and college years studying fine art and visual communications. I dutifully enrolled in Drawing I and Painting I, adding courses like 3D Design to my class schedule as my education progressed. But the one class that truly fascinated me, that stuck with me through all the years of trial and error, was Intro to Photography. I distinctly remember the first time I used a darkroom and was able to watch a black-and-white image emerge in the developing tray. It was pure magic!

Turned out that the Hipster Doofus has been right. With a camera in my hands, I could be an artist. What I came to love most about photography was that it was available to anyone (professional or amateur) who viewed the world with an aesthetic eye. It could even be used as a stop-motion, visual storytelling tool for the journalist in us all.

And so, spurred on by my fascination with light meters and f-stops, many years later, I earned a master's degree in photojournalism. I even managed to find quasi-gainful employment as a full-time newspaper photographer. (This was prior to the demise of real journalism as we once knew it.) In regard to photos and the process of making them, I have been pestering my friends, family and thousands of complete strangers with my camera ever since. At this point in my adult life, I have evolved into a source of true embarrassment to my daughter who refers to me as "just another weirdo taking pictures." Enough said.

Above:
Snapshot with Art Deco-style border, Pennsylvania road sign, 1930s.

```
To appreciate the irony of this turn of
events, you have to understand that I grew
up in a time when kids were rarely allowed
to touch the family camera, much less burn
through a roll of color film. Photography —
both the camera equipment required and the
materials needed to complete the printing
process — was expensive and precious.
```

Below:
Snapshot with deckled edge, view on a suspension bridge, taken from car's passenger seat, 1950s.

When my family piled into our Chevy Malibu for a very Brady-esque summer jaunt to the Wisconsin Dells or some other exotic destination, we would pull over to pose in front of landmarks, tourist traps or kitschy stores for our photo ops. My father would line up my brother and sister and me and take ONE PICTURE of us with his Kodak Instamatic. If somebody blinked or sneezed, he would skip the reshoot and just say something like, "Ah, I think we got it. Let's get back in the car. We don't want to waste the whole roll before we get to 'Tommy Bartlett's Water Show.'" It is for this reason that in many of my childhood photos, I am squinting into the blazing summer sun while saying "cheese" through gritted teeth or looking off-camera in a sweaty, confused daze.

In between our many nausea-inducing road trips (*Who's got the Dramamine?!*), my father bought me a portable typewriter as a belated birthday gift. It was tween-sized, not like the manual Royal model that he had used in the Army, the kind with the keys that got caught together in a clump if you typed too fast. My typewriter was white and robin's-egg blue and

Top:
Professional portrait, woman seated in the parlor, 1910s.
Photographs taken in ambient light in the home or work environment became more common as Americans embraced the inexpensive Kodak Brownie camera and the medium of photography itself during the early decades of the 20th century.

Middle:
Snapshot, group photo, 1920s.
On occasion, you may come across family photos that you can't identify. Who are these people? Where are they? What brought them together for this picture? Was lunch served? We may never know for sure. However, for me, the way the photographer chose to position the subjects was very telling and indicative of women's lives at that time. I personally like to call this snapshot "Can You Spot the Second-Class Citizens?" Feel free to come up with your own caption! It's fun!

Bottom:
Snapshot, two ladies wearing suits, posing with a sedan, 1940s.
What can I say? People LOVED their cars. Automobiles in photographs can help date an image. (Your favorite gearhead or vintage car owner can even look at something as small as a hood ornament or license plate and estimate what year a picture was taken.) You might need a psychic to tell you what happened to that back hubcap, though.

probably came from Sears, but it spoke to me nonetheless. I spent hours at the dining room table, typing and retyping paragraphs, tossing the carriage back with gusto after the bell dinged at the end of each line. I was practicing with a vengeance. I was like Katharine Hepburn on deadline, talking shop and trading barbs with the cigar-chompin' boys in the newsroom! *"No dice, Walter! I just got the facts from a strong-arm stooge in the getaway car! Stop the presses and find me a rewrite man!"*

One summer afternoon, when my father was en route to the TV with a sandwich in hand and the Sox game on his mind, he noticed me typing. With the commercial blaring in the other room, he knew he had a few minutes to spare for quality parenting, so he veered over and asked, "Whatcha writing, kid? Got a big scoop of some kind?" I barely looked up when I answered, "I'm going to write a book so I can make money. Then, I'm going to buy a camera so I can take all the pictures I want."

Was this the declaration of a petulant child? A single-minded pre-adolescent who hated being told what she could or couldn't do? Sure, I'll own up to both. As a young girl, I had already perfected a pouty face that would have put Winston Churchill to shame. But even back then, I knew that photography was the real deal. It provided the tiny, elegant details that gave any story its true staying power.

Above:
Snapshot, woman in fur-collared coat posing outside cathedral, 1920s.

```
Photography is an art form that has the
ability to lift the human spirit. Its visual
essence fires up the freewheeling, creative
right brain and connects it with analytical
science geek of the left brain. And then ...
BLAMMO! Ideas start percolating and miracles
can happen.
```

Below:
Snapshot, happy little girl jumping rope on the sidewalk near the front porch, 1930s. (The Great Depression? What's that? When I get tired of jumping, I'm gonna play jacks!)

There is a philosophy in the marketing world that suggests that if you share numbers and facts with your audience, they'll be informed. If you show them a picture, they'll remember. However, if you roll the information and the images together and tell a compelling story — as you can do with the pictures in your family photo album — you'll touch their hearts. And really, could there be anything more amazing than that?

Chapter 4: Where Did We Put That Old Shoebox?

"Do one thing every day that scares you."

— *Eleanor Roosevelt (1884-1962), First Lady of the United States and social advocate*

When I decided to start start digging around in my own family archive, I did have a recollection of some of the old photos that existed — my parents' wedding portrait, for example.

What I wasn't mentally prepared for were the odd snapshots of my family doing everyday things, wearing work-a-day clothes. I had forgotten about most of those, and I have to admit that they are priceless. The requisite pose-with-your-birthday-cake photos; the picture of my sister and her high-school friends, all wearing 501 Levis, standing with their arms linked on our front lawn one summer afternoon; the incredibly bad attempt I made at achieving a blow-dried, Farrah-Fawcett-style hairdo. It was all there, staring back at me, unflinchingly. My only regret is that I did not save more of my mugshots.

The beauty of using photography to start a dialogue with the next generation of women is that we all have these kinds of photos. Everybody has a box of disorganized prints and negatives or a couple of photo albums stashed away in a dark place. It's like we're all trying to hide the evidence. (In some cases, we are.)

No need to spend any money, just bring them out, ladies! Wave them like protest signs. Flaunt them like new tattoos. Recognize that they represent a historic tapestry, an intricate visual puzzle that will help you and yours understand how women got where we are today. Sure, you might stumble upon your old prom photo, a Kodak relic that'll make you laugh so hard that you pee in your pants, but that's a risk worth taking.

Chances are that during your formative years, a woman (or many women) did the heavy lifting in terms of your emotional and spiritual growth. Maybe it was your mother. Maybe it was your grandmother or aunt or neighbor or a family friend.

These were the homemakers and caregivers who mended the shirts and diapered the babies and washed millions of dishes. They were the self-trained medics

Above:
Snapshot, informal family photo, 1920s. This image reminds me of a social phenomenon that my father recalled from his childhood in Chicago during the 1930s. He said that Catholic families (like his) were large and mothers often had one baby right after another. In his words, it was common for "parents to send a new kid out to play every spring."

Previous Spread, Left:
Two of the crown jewels in the author's voluminous family archive.
Photograph by Kathleen Geraghty.

Previous Spread, Right:
Eleanor Roosevelt, head-and-shoulders portrait, facing front, circa 1945. Photograph. https://www.loc.gov/item/93503451/.

who took our temperatures and dispensed Bayer Aspirin or — God forbid — castor oil. They were the ones who packed the lunches, signed the report cards and forced us to have shame-based, religion-infused consciences, whether we liked it or not.

Of course, if your relations were women of some means and social standing, they employed people who tended to these tasks, so that they could focus on more refined pursuits like needlepoint or charity work or running high-class speakeasies. In wealthier circles, it was generally the woman's role to build relationships with the express intention of enhancing her family's — in particular, her husband's — standing in the community.

Some of our foremothers enjoyed long, happy and prosperous marriages, while others shouldered the burdens of poverty and abuse. Many came of age in a time of war or political unrest. Still others were born into more stable worlds of wealth and privilege, and as members of a higher class, had easy access to educational and cultural opportunities.

And yet, these incredibly diverse women had one thing in common: They set the stage for the next generation and made our time in the spotlight possible.

It's time to raise the curtain and let their stories see the light of day. You may say, "I don't have any really GOOD photos. We weren't exactly the Rockefellers. We weren't in *Life* magazine; we were just regular people. Half of our family photos are stuffed in a Wieboldt's shopping bag along with my Catholic school uniform."

Au contraire! While the images might not be organized or catalogued, what you undoubtedly do have are photos of women who DID IT ALL. They kept households and businesses running and they managed without the benefit of modern conveniences or timesaving devices. Whether they slaved over a hot stove all day or punched a timecard in order to bring home that bacon and fry it up in the pan, you can bet that they didn't get much rest. Not only that, they had to roll out of bed in the pitch dark when their wind-up alarm clocks went off at 5 a.m. Can you imagine not being able to hit a snooze button at least once? The unspeakable horror! The scary eye bags and facial puffiness!

Sorry, Missus. I Don't Understand You ...

It's also possible that some of the women in your family tree managed to accomplish all they did without being able to speak English. In the earliest decades of the 20th century, the immigrant population in the United States was on the rise. According to the Migration Policy Institute, the number

of foreign-born people living in America in 1900 was 10,341,300. By 1930, that number had climbed to 14,204,100 — almost 12 percent of the total U.S. population. Consider the challenge of negotiating a price with the local butcher when you have to make your case in a foreign language! How do you begin to convey the idea that you don't want the chicken head without looking like you are threatening that same butcher with decapitation?

Land Spreadin' Out So Far and Wide!

What constituted work back in the olden days was not necessarily easy or clean. Many previous generations of American families earned their living as farmers. This was a physically demanding job that lasted from dawn until dusk. Farm women cooked, cleaned, sewed, laundered clothing and linens, planted vegetable gardens and tended to livestock. They also raised children who, in turn, grew up to be the family's built-in labor force.

Farming as an occupation has been in steady decline in our country since the early 1800s, when industrialization brought a shift to specialized machinery, factories and mass production. According to United States Department of Agriculture, in 1900, farmers represented 38 percent of the U.S. labor force. By 1930, that number had fallen to 21 percent. In 1950, it hovered at 12 percent; in 1970, at 4.6 percent. By 1990, just 2.6 percent of all working Americans earned their living as farmers.

For urban women, work was equally taxing. If a lady earned a living outside the home in the early 20th century, she might very well have been employed in domestic service, or in a store or factory. The hours were long, working conditions often unsafe, and the pay was miniscule. Since the process of work itself (both in and outside the home) was more labor-

Above:
Left: Portrait, date and location unknown.
Right: Snapshot, older woman in house dress feeding the chickens,1930s.

Below:
United States Resettlement Administration, Lee, Russell, photographer. Woman at sewing machine in New York City tailor shop, United States, Nov. 1936. Photograph. https://www.loc.gov/item/2017734930/.

Above:
Left: Portrait, date and location unknown.
Right: Snapshot, bus riders, 1920s.

Below:
Snapshot, lady wearing cloche hat and fur-trimmed coat, late 1920s or early 1930s.

intensive than it is today, there was less time for lounging and for the average woman to contemplate her wants, needs, or innermost feelings. The size of her butt and the emergence of a new wrinkle took a back seat to more important things like paying the rent or mortgage and stretching whatever dollars happened to remain after that.

The Media and the Messages

Starting in the 1880s, mass-circulation magazines like *Harper's Bazaar*, *McCall's*, *Good Housekeeping*, *The Farmer's Wife* and *Vogue* did a thorough job of marketing "appropriate" styles of living to American women. (Some would call this an insidious form of brainwashing.) Authoritative articles offered tips on fashion, etiquette, cooking, cleaning, household budgeting, husband-pampering and raising well-bred, obedient children. For a much-needed break from reality, women could delve into Hollywood gossip and scandal via publications such as *Photoplay* and *Modern Screen* or the more salacious *Confidential*.

These ladies did not devote their teenage years to learning how to take a good selfie. If they wanted to check their look, they did so in a mirror, just like any self-respecting movie star was doing at that time. As a matter of fact, an average woman who snapped random photos of herself going about her day-to-day activities would have raised a few eyebrows. (Let's be perfectly clear: The word on the street would have been that she was insane.)

While the neighborhood grapevine might have conveyed local gossip with incredible speed and efficiency, if women were interested in national or world affairs, they got the scoop from mass media. All major stories and breaking news items were disseminated by way of daily newspapers or radio broadcasts. In densely populated urban areas, there were even morning and evening editions of the same newspaper, as well as foreign language weeklies that catered to various ethnic populations. However, the field of journalism was dominated by men in the early 20th century. This led to gatekeeping on the part of male reporters and editors, who dictated what stories relating to housewifery, shopping and society news would be covered on the "Women's Page," and how patriarchal in tone that coverage would be.

If a lady was able to afford a movie ticket, she might also catch a newsreel to learn about current events. What a treat for a cloistered female to *actually see* how people lived in other exotic parts of the globe! Her window to the world was opened even further in the late 1940s, when Americans began buying televisions for use in the home.

Run, Run, Get Around!

The introduction of the Ford Model T in 1908 brought major changes to American life. For workers, it ushered in a new era of assembly-line labor and mass production. For consumers, these automobiles were economic status symbols that offered spur-of-the-moment mobility and freedom. While rural families might have had access to a truck to use for errands, many urban women rode public transportation or walked to the local neighborhood businesses — grocery stores, butcher shops, bakeries, hardware stores, the "five-and-dimes," dress shops, tailors, milliners, shoemakers, and the like — for what they needed. Not every family could afford a car and the development of the Interstate Highway System didn't begin until the late 1950s, so people shopped where they lived.

That's Just the Tip of the Iceberg ...

As you'll discover in the pages ahead, these historical tidbits are quite eye-opening and can really help put the achievements of our foremothers into perspective. Keep in mind that you can always skate over the scandalous chapters in your family history if you choose to do so. (Nobody's on trial here, right?) However, before we get too deep into a discussion of what was happening in the world around these females who came before us, let's take a gander at what types of photos you will probably find in your family's own archive — or that forgotten, dusty shoebox on the top shelf of the closet.

Above:
Snapshot, woman relaxing with her feet in the sand, reading a copy of *College Humor* magazine, late 1920s or early 1930s.

Below:
Snapshot, ladies walking in town, 1930s.

You Never Know What You Might Find ... Prepare Yourself!

The possibilities are endless, but these types of images are the featured players in most family photo archives.

Daguerreotypes (1840s-1860s)

Introduced by the French inventor Louis Jacques Mandé Daguerre in Paris in 1839, the fragile daguerreotype was the first commercially successful photographic process. Daguerreotypes were very expensive, and therefore, available to only the upper classes. These one-of-a-kind images were made on mirror-like silver plates that were exposed to iodine fumes and mercury vapor. Once the smell cleared (Can you imagine?!), the resulting portrait was sealed behind glass in a decorative leather case, which was lined with silk or velvet to prevent scratches. Daguerreotypes were produced in a range of sizes, but most measured about 2 inches by 3 inches. A daguerreotype can look like a negative, a positive or a mirror image, depending on the angle from which it is viewed. (Some experts have compared the daguerreotype to a detailed hologram that changes from shiny to matte as it's rotated.) Tarnish around the edge of the image is normal. Due to the long exposure times (3-15 minutes) required for the earliest daguerreotypes, subjects had to remain completely still and expressionless during the photo session.

Ambrotypes/Collodion Positives (1850s-1880s)

The ambrotype, also known as the collodion positive, was created by bleaching the silver salts in a negative image and turning it into a positive image. (From a pop culture perspective, it was the photographic equivalent of being in "The Bizarro World" or "The Upside Down.") When displayed against a black background, the dark areas of the original negative appeared as highlights. The backing could be a piece of black velvet or a coating of black varnish, the latter of which was a popular technique used in inexpensive photo studios. Though the ambrotype/collodian positive was actually a glass negative, its emulsion was too thin to use for printing purposes. These types of images were relatively inexpensive to produce. They became popular with open-air photographers because portraits could be cranked out in a few minutes while customers waited.

Top:
Daguerreotype image without case. Detroit Publishing Co., Publisher. Seated Woman. Photograph. https://www.loc.gov/item/2016817070/.

Bottom:
Ambrotype/Collodion positive. Subject and date unknown. Collection of the author. Photograph by Kathleen Geraghty.

Opposite Page:
Selected items from my family archive. (Can you tell we like to keep *everything*?) Photograph by Kathleen Geraghty.

Top:
Ferrotype/Tintype, sleeve stamped "Potters Patent March 7, 1865."

Bottom:
Carte de visite, 1890s, inscribed on back
"Mary Haley Hawes
b. 1840 - Oct. 12
m. 1863 - Oct. 14
d. 1903 - Oct. 5"

Opposite Page:
Albumen print; studio portrait of woman and children; mounted on cardstock and hand-trimmed, 1870s.

Ferrotypes/Tintypes (1850s-1900s)

In the ferrotype process, an underexposed negative image was produced on a thin iron plate. The picture was darkened with paint, lacquer or enamel and coated with photographic emulsion, giving the negative the appearance of a positive image. Ferrotypes were similar in size to the high-end daguerreotype, but were much less detailed, making them a more affordable option for consumers. Commonly known as tintypes (possibly because tin shears were used to cut the photographic plates), these images were popular with Civil War soldiers, immigrants and working-class people. Ferrotypes/tintypes were often produced by sidewalk photographers at parks, fairs, carnivals and beaches. The finished images were placed in decorative cardboard or paper sleeves to give them more appeal as souvenirs.

Albumen Prints (1850s-1900s)

The albumen print was invented in 1850 and remained the most common type of photographic print for the next 40 years. As gross as it sounds, an albumen print was made by coating a piece of paper with a layer of egg white and salt to create a smooth surface. (Hash browns were extra.) The egg goop was then coated with silver nitrate, which made the salts light-sensitive. A glass negative was placed on top of the whole mess and exposed to the sun to produce a print. Amazingly, this process resulted in a highly detailed image that was relatively stable and fixed. Albumen prints ranged in size from one square inch to 20 by 20 inches. Upon close inspection, the emulsion in these ultra-thin prints often shows signs of cracking or a color shift toward the sepia range. Individual paper fibers in high-quality albumen prints can be seen with a magnifying glass. Another factor called "silvering," in which a glowing or pooling effect occurs in the dark areas of the photograph, can signal that the print is albumen.

Carte de Visites (1850s-1910s)

During the mid-19th century, the carte de visite became a popular use of the albumen print method. These images were approximately 3.5 inches by 2 inches — the size of a formal calling card — and were pasted onto cardboard mounts. The typical carte de visite was created in a studio setting, with the subject often holding a prop like a book, a fan or a badass firearm! Carte de visites utilized the multiple-print production process (as opposed to earlier one-of-a-kind daguerreotypes), which made them inexpensive. As a result, they were popular during the Civil War with both Union and Confederate soldiers who wanted to leave mementos behind for their loved ones. Early carte de visites had thin, lightweight mounts and square corners. By the 1870s, thicker cardboard stock was used for the mounting process and rounded corners became popular.

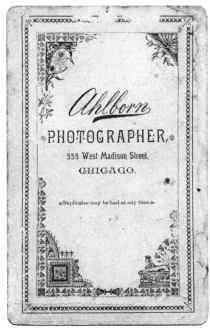

Cabinet Cards (1860s-1910s)

Cabinet cards were essentially a bigger, flashier version of the humble carte de viste. These formal photographic portraits measured approximately 4 inches by 6 inches and were pasted on thick, rigid cardboard. As the name suggested, they were just the right size to be displayed in a place of prominence — such as in a lovely cabinet in the parlor. The front of the cabinet card featured a bottom border where the photographer's name and logo were printed. The back was often decorated with an elaborate printed or embossed design and a repeat of the studio's contact info. By the 1880s, cabinet cards were mounted on various types of cardboard (as opposed to just the standard cream color), and were accented with gold or silver lettering and bevelled edges. Size variations such as the boudoir card (5 inches by 8 inches) and the imperial mount (7 inches by 10 inches) began to appear around this time as well. The cabinet card's popularity dwindled after the turn of the century, particularly after the real photographic postcard (RPPC) was introduced.

This Spread:
Above: Cabinet cards, back and front sides. Astrom Photographic Art Studio, Brockton, Massachusetts; and Ahlborn Photographer, Chicago, Illinois.

Opposite Page: Cabinet card, front side. Ahlborn Photographer, Chicago, Illinois.

Above:
Snapshot, silver-gelatin print, 1920s.
Labeled on back, "Taken down by the lake."

Below:
Snapshot, chromogenic print, dated 1965.
(Great vibe, even in black and white!)

Silver-Gelatin Prints (1870s-present)

Introduced in the 1870s, the silver-gelatin print quickly became the go-to standard in photographic printing processes. It utilized a new type of paper that was coated with gelatin containing light-sensitive silver salts. The magical end result was an image that was more stable and did not turn yellow with age. By 1895, silver-gelatin prints had kicked the old-school albumen prints to the curb, primarily because were easier to produce. Though not as thin as albumen prints, the early silver-gelatin images were also very lightweight. Around the 1930s, the heavier weight of silver-gelatin photo paper became the norm and it remains the standard for black-and-white photography today. Unlike albumen prints, the paper fibers in these types of images cannot be seen with a magnifying device. Early silver-gelatin images were full bleed — meaning they extended to the edge of the photo paper — but white borders began to appear in the 1910s. While these images could be affixed to heavier, rigid cardboard (as in the case of some cabinet cards), most were unmounted.

Real Photo Postcards/RPPCs (1900s-1940s)

Photographs that were printed on actual postcard stock were relatively inexpensive, hugely popular and could be used for many purposes, including holiday greetings, birthday wishes or travel souvenirs. Real photo postcards (often called RPPCs) were frequently given to family members for inclusion in an album. Whether the sender was living in the same house or an ocean away in the old country, postcards were a sure-fire way to say you cared. The use of the word "POST CARD" was granted by the U.S. government to private printers in 1901. The first cards were called "Private Mailing Cards." The familiar divided-back postcard — with the address quadrant on the right and space for a handwritten message on the left — began to appear in 1907. The earliest postcard photographs were full-bleed images, but white borders began to appear circa 1915.

Chromogenic Prints (1930s-present)

Also called a C-type print or dye coupler print, this type of image is printed from a color negative or transparency. Most of the color photos in any family archive are chromogenic prints. These images contain three emulsion layers of light-sensitive silver salts — red, blue and green. The light-sensitive material in the print, similar to what is found in black-and-white photographic papers, is a silver-halide emulsion. Chromogenic prints are far more delicate than black-and-white images. After World War II, color snapshots became very popular. These older color photos will fade or turn yellow with age, particularly if they are framed and exposed to sunlight or stored in areas that have extreme temperature fluctuations. Early color

Left:
Real Photo Postcard, studio portrait, 1920s.

Above:
Real Photo Postcard, early 1900s. This one falls under the category of "Can You Believe What People Do to Their Children?"

Below:
Color Slides, storage box and viewing loupe, 1980s. Photographers took exposed rolls of 35mm slide film to labs for processing. In return, they received individually mounted slides packaged in small storage boxes. Ektachrome, shown here, was a high-speed slide film that was first sold in the 1940s.

photos were printed on fiber-based papers, which feel less plastic to the touch than color images that were produced after the late 1960s.

Color Slides (1935-present)

Guess what? Those little 2-inch by 2-inch color images that have cardboard or plastic mounts are called slides, or reversal film! Not to be confused with 35mm film negatives, color slides are a positive image on a transparent base. While this technology had been evolving for nearly two decades, it wasn't until Eastman Kodak introduced its Kodachrome color reversal film in 1935 that slides really took off with the general public. Slides were intended for projection onto a large screen, so groups of people could sit together in the dark and be bored by out-of-focus vacation photos. The colors seen

Above:
Snapshot, silver-gelatin print, 1947. Faded, darkened and sun-damaged image, cracked emulsion, stained, covered in schmutz and fingerprints. Possibly burned with a stray cigarette. (This is an example of an image that was neglected and stored in heinous conditions. Don't let this happen to your precious photos!)

in slide images were generally very vibrant, but it took a somewhat skilled (or lucky) photographer to capture them. Slide film was less forgiving than negative film in terms of requiring correct exposure. Underexposed slide images look too dark, while overexposed slides look too light. Making actual prints from slide film was also more costly than making them from color negatives.

Polaroids (1947-present)

This magical, self-developing photographic process, also known as a dye diffusion transfer print, was invented in 1947 by Edwin Land, an American scientist. The earliest Polaroid cameras used a chemical pod and two film rolls that were sandwiched together during the developing process. Later versions were sold with pack films that featured eight or 10 images. After shooting a Polaroid, the photographer pulled the film out of the camera, then peeled the positive image apart from the negative at the end of the developing process. Sometimes people just couldn't wait 60 whole seconds to see their pictures — which is why Polaroids can have streaks or splotches across the face of the image. The Polaroid camera was heavily marketed in the 1960s (one model pitched to young consumers was called "The Swinger") and eventually became a visual tool embraced by students and fine artists. By the early 1970s, Polaroid technology had evolved so that after the individual image was ejected from the camera, people could watch as the picture developed right before their eyes. Cosmic, man!

Right:
Polaroid instant photograph, 1960s. Woman in the kitchen, using wall-mounted rotary telephone.

(Do you love this lady or what? Didn't we all know someone like this when we were growing up? This was a cheerful woman whose everyday ensemble was a kitchen smock and a smile, a gal whose to-do list was never-ending. She might have been your mother, your aunt or a neighbor, but wasn't she fantastic? Note proximity of ashtray to phone. This was obviously the command center in her home!)

Did You Wash Your Hands?

Top Five Tips for Handling Antique or Vintage Photographs, Negatives and Slides

1) Water, coffee and beverages are a definitely a Bozo No-No. Even a few beads of moisture on the emulsion of a photograph can cause it to stick to images stacked on top of it and ruin it for good. Wipe your table down and dry it completely before spreading out any archival images. Large rolls of white craft paper can also be used to create a pristine workspace. If you want to cocktail it up while you peruse the family photos, keep your drinks on a side table and use a Sippy Cup.

2) Never write on the back of an old photo. The pressure of using a ballpoint pen can actually dent fragile prints, making handwriting visible from the front of the image. Ink can also smear. Instead, use a soft lead pencil to very lightly write a small reference number on the back edge of a photo and then create a separate caption/data notebook or spreadsheet.

3) Kids definitely need to see these photos and hear the stories that go with them. But, their jelly fingers are, like liquids, a disaster waiting to happen when it comes to pictures. To ensure that none of your vintage portraits get run over by a speeding Big Wheel, gummed by a teething infant, or flushed down the toilet in a spur-of-the-moment science experiment, adult supervision is a must if the little people are going to participate.

4) Inexpensive cotton inspection gloves, available at craft and discount stores, are helpful for keeping your vintage images free of fingerprints and smudges. They also make it easy to hold negatives and slides up to the light for viewing. Cotton gloves are used in a variety of industries and art-related occupations and are wonderful to have around if you plan on committing any future felonies.

5) Humidity, high temperatures and light are the enemies! Keep your photos in a dank basement and you risk mold or pest infiltration. Keep your photos in the 120-degree attic and you risk fading, curling, warping and cracking. A good rule of thumb is to store your photos a cool, dark place that will preserve the emulsions and pigments. If you wouldn't curl up for a quick nap in the space, don't stash your family photos there.

✳ ✳ ✳

Chapter 5:
The Cost of Photography:
Lookin' Good (If We Can Afford It)

"People say that money is not the key to happiness, but I always figured if you have enough money, you can have a key made."

— *Joan Rivers (1933-2014), American comedian, actress, writer and TV host*

As you start excavating the past in your family archive, the first thing that becomes evident is that, at the dawn of the 20th century, photography was primarily used to commemorate life's milestones. When diplomas were earned or wedding bells rang, consumers would clean up, spiff up and head to the local photographer's studio to pose for a very somber and formal portrait.

Everyday life was not frequently documented due to the considerable expense involved in creating these early images. While photography's roots can be traced back to the work of French inventors Joseph Nicéphore Niépce circa 1826 and Jacques Louis Mandé Daguerre circa 1839, it wasn't until the introduction of Kodak's Brownie Camera in 1900 that the medium became truly affordable and accessible.

Technological advancements turned the camera into both a tool and an amusement for the masses. A new photographic aesthetic also emerged in the form of the do-it-yourself snapshot. Industrialization and urban growth my have helped define the "American Century," but it was the portable camera that captured every madcap moment for posterity.

Vigorous marketing campaigns by Eastman Kodak encouraged families to shoot photos without being overly concerned about producing high-quality images. With a retail price of one dollar and catchy slogans like "You press the button, we do the rest," the Brownie was irresistible. It sold so well, that by 1905, one third of all American households had a camera.

The result was that photography as an art form became more experimental and playful. The days of rigid studio portraits gave way to a new era defined by joyful group photos, souvenir travel images and snapshots that captured the spirit of a new way of living. And you can bet that if a lady was going to dress up and step out, she wanted a picture of her outfit!

A Look at Her Life in Pictures: 1900-1950

The Baby Photo (Cute as a Button and Wearing a Party Dress)

A Precious Baby Girl might have had a solo portrait session at a local studio. Or, she might have been photographed along with her Sainted Mother, who had birthed another child at home right after 6 a.m. Mass, but before starching her husband's shirts for the week.

The School Portrait (Beauty and Brains Combined!)

While group photos of an entire class were common, individual studio portraits were generally taken to commemorate grade school and/or high school graduation. In the former, the Female Student will look awkward and self-conscious. In the latter, aloof yet alluring.

The Religious Ceremony (Say a Little Prayer for Me)

First Holy Communion, Sacrament of Confirmation, Bat Mitzvah: These were serious and somber occasions. At least, that's what her parents told her. She is a God-Fearing, Pure and Spiritual Young Lady.

The Wedding Portrait (The Main Event)

When wedding vows were swapped, cameras were on hand to pay homage to The Virgin Bride in all her glory. The formal wedding portrait is, by far, the most common type of photograph found in most family archives. Additional candid images taken by professional and amateur photographers capture the minute details and triumphant spirit of her wedding day. Jackpot Bingo! She caught a MAN!

The Snapshot (Home, Work, Travel and Just Plain Fun!)

Snapshots were photographs that were "shot" spontaneously and quickly, often without artistic or journalistic intent. As a result, these slice-of-life pictures may be poorly exposed, out of focus or oddly composed — but that's what makes them cool! As the use of portable cameras increased, informal snapshots became run-of-the-mill, and the full range of women's daily activities were preserved on film for posterity. (Here she is baking the cake, here she is serving it — and now she's washing the dishes! She is a talented and multifaceted gal!)

This Spread:
Above, Top: Portrait, baby girl, 1910s.
Above, Bottom: Portrait, baby girl, 1930s.
Opposite Page:
Top: Graduation portraits, 1900s and 1930s.
Bottom: Class photo, 1920s.

Previous Spread:
Left: Wedding portrait, early 1900s.
Right: Snapshot, flower girls, 1940s.

Why Weren't More Photos Taken in Grandma's Day?

A family's disposable income was dictated not only by the earning capacity of its members, but by the political and economic climates of the time. In addition to the turmoil of World War I, America experienced several economic recessions between 1900 and 1927. These downturns paled in comparison to the rampant joblessness and poverty experienced during the Great Depression, when even upper middle-class families struggled to make ends meet. Shortly thereafter, World War II brought about the rationing of food, gas and clothing and a call for Americans to donate whatever funds they could spare to support the military effort.

In the early 20th century, the United States was also shifting from an agrarian to an industrial society. Visiting a photographer's studio was easier, from a purely geographic standpoint, for those who lived in or near an urban population center. However, when the rent was late or you were in need of butter-and-egg money, having a high-end family portrait made would have been an unthinkable luxury. This type of financial reality, of course, added to the considerable appeal of snapshot photography.

This Page:
Left: Cabinet card, wedding portrait, Nemecek Studio, Chicago, 1910s.

Right: Studio portrait, bride and groom, 1930s. (Note escape door at the right, just in case either of them had a last-minute change of heart.)

Opposite Page:
Top Left: Portrait, First Holy Communion girl with candle and rosary, dated 1921.

Top Right: Portrait, First Holy Communion girl with mother, late 1900s or early 1910s.

Bottom: Portrait, wedding party photographed in the studio, 1920s.

United States Population Characteristics: A Quick Overview
U.S. Census Totals for 1900-1950 (In Millions)

Census	Total	Male	Female	White	Black	Urban	Rural
1900	75.9	38.8	37.1	66.8	9.1	30.2	45.9
1910	91.9	47.3	44.6	81.7	10.2	42.0	50.1
1920	105.7	53.9	51.8	94.8	10.8	54.2	51.7
1930	122.7	62.1	60.6	110.2	12.4	69.1	54.0
1940	131.6	66.0	65.6	118.2	13.4	74.7	57.4
1950	150.6	74.8	75.8	134.9	15.7	96.8	54.4

Source: U.S. Census Bureau, U.S. Census of Population: 1940, Vol. II, Part 1, and Vol. IV, Part 1; 1950, Vol. II, Part 1; 1960, Vol. I, Part 1; 1970, Vol. I, Part B; Current Population Reports, P25-1095 and P25-1130; and "Resident Population of the United States: Estimates, by Sex, Race, and Hispanic Origin, with Median Age"; release date: December 28, 1998. (Starting in 1960, Americans were able to self-identify with multiple races, as opposed to having the census taker decide for them and categories beyond "white" and "black" became standard.)

Adding It Up

However, it's clear that even in tough times families were willing to scrape up enough money to get their photos taken when the occasion warranted it. Creative budgeting and penny pinching certainly helped finance many of the fabulous vintage portraits that exist in our family archives today.

While government figures are not available for every year between 1900 and 1950, scholarly resources can shed light on how much disposable income the average family might have had during those five decades. Some university-based studies offer glimpses of early 20th century life in cities like New York or Boston, providing specifics on union wages, apartment rents, or even the cost of a pack of cigarettes. Academic researchers frequently studied areas with large, diverse populations, where subjects were plentiful, as opposed to small-town America and rural regions.

It's important to note that during World War I, the Great Depression and World War II, government funds were allocated for the military, domestic infrastructure improvements and social service efforts, as opposed to sophisticated data collection and assessment. These numbers were also tallied without the benefit of digital technology. In other words, teams of actual people with pencils did the counting and the math, and the whole process was incredibly labor-intensive.

As a matter of fact, something as simple as determining the number of Americans who were unemployed in 1933 — the year generally recognized as the nadir of the Great Depression — will often yield conflicting results. (While it's frequently estimated that nearly 25 percent of the population was jobless during that bleak year in our history, some sources put it as high as 30 percent.) With all these caveats in mind, please take a moment to absorb the following information.

This Page:
Top: Baby Brownie Special; original retail price of $1.25 circa 1939.
Bottom: Brownie Reflex Synchro Model; original retail price of $6.00 circa 1946.

Photographs by Kathleen Geraghty. Camera model info courtesy of the George Eastman Legacy Collection, George Eastman Museum, Rochester, New York.

According to the U.S. Department of Labor, Bureau of Labor Statistics at www.bls.gov:

- 1900 — Average annual household income = $750
    ($22,548 in 2019 dollars)
- 1918 — Average annual household income = $1,518
    ($25,690 in 2019 dollars)
- 1934 — Average annual household income = $1,524
    ($29,063 in 2019 dollars; unemployment and prices increase during the 1930s while income stays relatively flat)
- 1950 — Average annual household income = $4,237
    ($44,927 in 2019 dollars)

Source: 100 Years of U.S. Consumer Spending: Data for the Nation, New York City, and Boston. Report 991, May 2006.

Opposite Page:
Snapshot, Springfield, Massachusetts, military parade day, late 1910s.

Prices of selected items in 1913:

- Potatoes, 2.5 cents/pound
- Flour, 3.3 cents/pound
- Rice, 8.7 cents/pound
- White bread, 5.6 cents/pound
- Round steak, 22.3 cents/pound
- Butter, 38.3 cents/pound
- No. 1 Kodak Brownie Camera, $1.00*

Prices of selected items in 1934:

- Potatoes, 1.7 cents/pound
- Flour, 5.1 cents/pound
- Rice, 8.1 cents/pound
- White bread, 8.3 cents/pound
- Round steak, 27.4 cents/pound
- Butter, 35.4 cents/pound
- Bituminous coal, $8.36/ton
- Kodak Baby Brownie Camera, $1.00 to $1.25*
- No. 2C Kodak Brownie Camera, $4.00*

Prices of selected items in 1947:

- Apples, 12.8 cents/pound
- Potatoes, 5.0 cents/pound
- Bananas, 15 cents/pound
- Flour, 4.8 cents/pound
- Rice 18.4 cents/pound
- White bread 12.5 cents/pound
- Round steak 75.6 cents/pound
- Milk, 18.7 cents/quart
- Butter, 80.5 cents/pound
- Kodak Brownie Flash Six-20 Camera, $6.00*

Above:
Real Photo Postcards (RPPCs)
Top, 1920s; Bottom, 1930s.
RPPCs created in small photo studios and local arcades were a relatively inexpensive way to have a portrait made.

Source: Stephen B. Reed, "One hundred years of price change: the Consumer Price Index and the American inflation experience," Monthly Labor Review, U.S. Bureau of Labor Statistics, April 2014, https://doi.org/10.21916/mlr.2014.14.

*Camera prices: compiled from print advertisements of the time period.

Family Snapshots: A Slice of Life

After the introduction of the Kodak Brownie Camera in 1900, snapshot photography became extremely popular. A portable (and affordable) camera could now help average Americans document their everyday activities in casual settings. Most snapshots were taken outdoors in daylight, as consumer cameras with flash synchronization would not surface until the late 1930s and flashbulbs would not become commonplace until the 1940s.

However, given the prices that American consumers paid for the necessities of daily living, it's apparent that photography — in any form, whether professional or amateur — was still something of a luxury in the early decades of the 20th century.

Top:
Snapshot, group of young people outdoors, late 1910s or early 1920s.

Middle:
Snapshot, woman seated in wicker chair with two children, 1930s.

Bottom:
Snapshot, siblings on the first day of school, Earlimart, California, dated 1936.

Chapter 6:
Home, Heart, Head

"And the day came when the risk to remain tight in a bud was more painful than the risk it took to blossom."

—Anaïs Nin (1903-1977), French essayist and memoirist

I have come to realize that there are four components to a woman's day-to-day existence and her general well-being or lack thereof. They are as follows:

- What's going on in her Home
- What's going on in her Heart
- What's going on in her Head
- Chocolate: Is it accessible when needed?

You might have your own ideas about what constitutes feminine existence and that's perfectly fine. We are each our own unique brand of lady-bird!

My point here is that women are defined and motivated by what is currently happening in their Homes, their Hearts and their Heads. As a gender, women are intellectual and inventive, empathetic and energetic, nurturing and no-nonsense. Women possess an emotional intelligence that allows them to tackle problems effectively. Truth be told, we often do so with fewer resources at our disposal than those available to our male counterparts. As it has often been said about Ginger Rogers, the legendary RKO movie actress and dancer, she did everything her co-star Fred Astaire did, but she did it backwards and in high heels.

Like us, our female ancestors lived in uncertain times. They faced dilemmas and challenges, sometimes landing in a whole mess of trouble. And yet, when people turned to them for help, these women managed to soldier on, caring for their elders, raising children, cooking, cleaning and nursing the sick. It didn't matter whether home was on the farm or in the city; there was always plenty of work to be done. Yet, somehow, these women also managed to study, plan, build, laugh, love and pray so that subsequent generations could benefit from their efforts.

While analyzing your female ancestors' lives, you might utilize this Home-Heart-Head model of inquiry. Approach their lives by starting with the external, community and societal forces (Home) that impacted them; consider the people they loved and cared for in

Above:
Snapshot, informal group portrait, 1920s.

Opposite Page:
Top: Outdoor candid group portrait inscribed "More Church Members," 1910s.

Bottom Left: Family portrait, Imada Studio, Los Angeles, California, dated on back "August 20, 1937."

Bottom Right: Snapshot, three ladies posing in the back yard, 1940s.

Previous Spread:
Left: Studio portrait with ripped and cracked emulsion, 1910s.

Right: Carte de viste, stamped "Calvert Bros. & Taylor; Cor. Cherry & Union Sts., Nashville," late 1890s or early 1900s.

the midst of the world in which they lived (Heart); and whether they were able to pursue an education or career (Head) or explore their own desires and interests (a supercharged combo of Heart /Head.) With the "Three H's" in mind, I invite you to give thought to these questions as you attempt to imagine and revisit a particular woman's life through photographs:

Home

- Was she born in an urban or a rural area?
- Did she live in a community with people who were similar to her and her family? Or, was she an outsider of sorts?
- What kind of house/apartment/shared environment did she live in?
- Who did she live with at different times in her life? (Parents, siblings, husband/partner, children, other relatives or friends)
- What were the social and cultural rules and rituals of the day?
- Did religion play a role in her life? In her home? In her community?
- Could she leave home unchaperoned? Could she do so at night?
- Did she have access to public transportation?
- Could she drive an automobile?
- What was the economic situation in her childhood home?
- Did her financial situation improve or decline as she matured?
- What was the state of the world in which she came of age? What global or national issues were important to her family/community?

Heart

- What did she dream about or aspire to become?
- Did she have any people or systems in place to protect her, love her and keep her safe from worry and danger?
- What did she do for fun? How much leisure time did she have?
- What were the rules of courtship and dating in her youth?
- Did she fall in love? (Maybe even more than once?)
- Was birth control discussed or even available when she was a young woman? What happened in the case of an unexpected pregnancy?

Head

- Was education readily available to her? Did she access it?
- Was she able to vote? Did she hold any particular political views?
- Could she have a career if she wanted one?
- What employment options were available to her throughout the various stages of her life?
- Was she ever allowed to live or travel on her own as an independent woman in pursuit of her career or educational goals?

More Church Members

Pop Quiz!

Let's pretend that you find this wonderful cabinet card in your family archive. You might not know this young woman's name, but how much can you determine from looking at her photo?

1. **This portrait was made to commemorate her:**
   - Formal debut into society as a desirable young lady
   - Grade school commencement after finishing the eighth grade
   - Prize-winning pickle entry at the Illinois State Fair
   - Desire to get out of the house that day and do something different

2. **Her dress and shoes were purchased for the occasion.**
   - True or False or Maybe

3. **She traveled to the photographer's studio by way of:**
   - A horse and carriage
   - Elevated train or streetcar
   - A Ford Model T
   - A donkey, just like the Blessed Virgin Mary

4. **She is wearing a corset in this photograph.**
   - True or False or Maybe

5. **If she comes home from this photo session and announces that she has realized she would like to continue her education and become a doctor, her mother will:**
   - Immediately seek her husband's counsel on this troubling matter
   - Weep and carry on about her daughter's lack of humility and disinterest in all things feminine and relating to home and family
   - Call the convent and ask the nuns to immediately come and get her daughter who is clearly out of hand and has lost her mind
   - Faint and wet her pants (or her voluminous bloomers, to be exact)

Check the Answers!

1. All signs point to this being a grade school graduation portrait, created in the early 1900s. However, it's also possible that this girl might have known how to make a fabulous Kosher dill pickle.

2. Her dress dates to close to 1905 and her shoes to about 1909. The latter appear a bit too large for her and are already broken-in, suggesting that they were borrowed for the photo or were hand-me-downs.

3. The Ford Model T was introduced in October 1908. If this portrait was made prior to that, the other options were viable for her transportation to the photo studio.

4. Circa 1900-1910, when a young lady entered her early teens, it was time to start wearing a corset. This undergarment was thought to help create an attractive figure and graceful posture. For propriety's sake, it was a mother's duty to introduce her young daughter to her first corset. Teenage girls often slept in them at night in order to "train" their waistlines to measure as little as 15 inches in circumference.

5. In the early 1900s, a woman was expected to defer to her husband on all important matters and to focus primarily on the issues pertaining to the home. This included the raising of children, who were supposed to be well-mannered and respectful. In a middle-class household, a young lady who expressed an interest in pursuing a career — as opposed to catching a suitable husband — would have been viewed as headstrong and something of a wild card. If she dared to dream of a career in medicine, she would have been encouraged to become a nurse, not a doctor. (In 1905, only 4 percent of all medical school graduates were women.)

Chapter 7:
Let's Take It One Decade at a Time

"It took me quite a long time to develop a voice, and now that I have it, I am not going to be silent."

—Madeleine Albright (1937-), America's first female Secretary of State

My Fair Ladies: If you've come this far in your own "Thanks to Her" project, you are obviously in it to win it! I'm impressed with your bravery and willingness to dig deep into the past. However, once you have unearthed your family's archive and discovered a cornucopia of photographs and ephemera, you may have questions. The most common among them being: *"Who's gonna clean up this mess?"* Issues of general housekeeping and indentured servitude aside, it is difficult to assess the full importance of your family photos without putting them into some type of historical context.

In addition to the format of the individual photographs, there are many visual clues that can help you pinpoint what was happening in a woman's life and in her world at the time a particular image was created. Among them are:

- Types of clothing, accessories and jewelry
- Hairstyles and makeup trends
- Automobiles, buses, trains and airplanes
- Forms of technology in homes and businesses
- Architecture (private homes, public buildings)
- Signage (advertising, storefronts, road signs)
- Printed media (newspapers, magazines).

The photographs in this chapter have been organized by decade. Keep in mind that this process is not an exact science. At first glance, it would appear that the subject's attire might provide enough visual detail to accurately date a photo. This is not always the case.

While some women had the extra coinage to be able to adopt the latest fashions, others might have lacked the ability to replace their old clothing. A lady's hairstyle is often a better indicator of the year in which a photo was taken; changing her "do" was a simple and cost-effective way to be chic.

Additionally, if a girl was raised in a conservative environment, she would not have been permitted to gallivant around in daring, modern ensembles that showcased her sparkling personality — or her cleavage.

This Page:
Top: Studio portrait, 1910s.
Bottom: Snapshot, 1930s.
Opposite Page:
Top: Faculty portrait, Earlimart, CA, 1930.
Left: Snapshot, nurse in uniform, 1920s.
Right: Snapshot, labor protest, 1960s.
Previous Spread:
Left: Studio portrait, 1920s.
Right: Snapshot, woman in parlor, 1940s.

Societal and political forces also impacted a woman's wardrobe. For example, you might find a photo that features an Art Deco-influenced 1930s border, but notice that the subjects are wearing clothing from the late 1920s. Economic hardships often compelled women and girls to recycle outfits that were clearly "last season," or in the meanest and leanest of times, made of no-frills sackcloth. *(Why throw that patterned flour sack away when we can sew a perfectly lovely house dress out of it?)* When World War II made rationing a necessity, inventive women even altered secondhand men's suits to make ensembles for themselves.

Modes of transportation seen in various photos will help illustrate the enormous impact that early 20th century industrialization had on the lives of average American women. As electricity lit up their world, the automobile, train and airplane helped them explore it. The telephone connected them to others, both near and far. Radio, print media and advertising helped them keep their fingers on the pulse of what was cutting-edge. This increase in the flow of information also made women keenly aware of new opportunities — and gave birth to previously unimaginable goals and aspirations.

The summaries of the decades that follow also feature events that helped shape women's lives. The achievements of female artists, writers, activists, athletes, scholars, inventors and businesswomen are highlighted, though in the interest of making this book shorter than the Bible, I could not include them all. These factoids and figures are simply an overview of the past. I hope they will inspire you to do further research into the areas that interest you most.

In examining the years between 1900 and 1950, images of American women as caregivers, tireless workers, and stewards of the country's moral compass emerge quite frequently. These were the mothers, sisters, daughters, grandmothers, aunts, teachers, social workers, nurses, farm and factory laborers, waitresses, maids, cooks, clerks, and altruistic neighbors who diligently kept the wheels of our nation turning. Overlooked and underestimated, they generally took a back seat to white men in the pages of American history.

Luckily, through the magic that is photography, we still have all their brilliance and spirit preserved on film. And luckily for American women, while being demure and soft-spoken were qualities that were thrust upon them by the social mores of the day, they were never voiceless. There was always a tribe of free-thinking rabble-rousers who liked nothing better than to speak up on behalf of their fellow sisters. They came from various rungs of the socioeconomic ladder, but they had one thing in common: They didn't take any crap from anybody. God bless 'em all.

1900s: New Ideas, New Technologies and The New Woman

"I had to make my own living and my own opportunity. But I made it! Don't sit down and wait for the opportunities to come. Get up and make them."

—*Madame C.J. Walker (1867-1919), African-American businesswoman and philanthropist*

At the dawn of the 20th century, Americans witness an increase in social feminism. Whether motivated by the electric lights that lengthen their days, or the popular Ragtime music of the era, middle-class females are fired up and itching to get out of the house.

In urban areas, they can ride trolleys to visit friends on the other side of town. They can venture out at night (with a chaperone, of course) since the illuminated streets are no longer a frightening place to be. They also join women's associations in huge numbers. This work allows them to advocate for social reforms while not requiring them to be unladylike by addressing the bigger issue of women's rights. Talk about the elephant in the room ...

In contrast, the more radical "New Woman" asserts a public presence through work, education, politics and anything else that does not align with Victorian ideals. These ladies embrace youth, mobility, freedom and independent thinking. If a woman is bold enough to publicly support birth control or criticize the patriarchal family structure, she is considered an extremist, a troublemaker, and a threat to decency!

Women are gaining independence in an America that has become an undisputed global power. It is the world's largest agricultural producer, with crops distributed cross-continent by five railroad systems. The nation's oil wells fuel the petroleum industry and the United States is the world's top producer of steel, a material that is key to the expansion of urban areas. Telephones allow for instant communication of ideas and are changing the very fabric of American life.

The Progressive Era, which started in the 1890s, is picking up steam and various efforts are being made to improve American society as a whole. Women are lobbying (some more visibly and loudly than others) for many of these developments.

Amazingly, American women are able to do all these things while wearing rib-crunching corsets and stepping gingerly around piles of horse dung in the carriage-filled streets.

Above:
Studio portrait, late 1890s or early 1900s.

Opposite Page, Top:
Studio group portrait with decorative mat, late 1890s or early 1900s.

Previous Spread, Left:
Du Bois, W. E. B. , Collector, Askew, Thomas E., 1850?-1914, photographer. Four African-American women seated on steps of building at Atlanta University, Georgia. [1899 or 1900] Photograph. https://www.loc.gov/item/95507126/.

Previous Spread, Right:
Studio portrait, cabinet card, early 1900s.

1900 — That's My Property, Dude!

Starting in the 1830s, the concept that females could actually think, work and manage money outside of the confines marriage begins to take root. Many men find these notions troubling, sensing that a lady with her own nest egg might eventually flee the nest. However, by 1900, every state in the union has passed some version of a Married Women's Property Act. Prior to these forms of legislation, upon marriage, a newly-minted "Missus" lost her legal rights to earning wages, collecting rents, owning or selling properties or filing lawsuits. American women are now fortunate in that they are no longer forced to relinquish these rights to their husbands.

1900 — Photography Is a Snap for Everyone

In February, the Eastman Kodak Company debuts The Brownie Camera — a sweetheart of a deal for consumers. The camera is essentially a simple leatherette-covered cardboard box that takes 2.25-inch pictures on roll film. It has no viewfinder, but provides "sighting lines" on the top to help the photographer compose an image. With The Brownie Camera's $1 retail price and user-friendly mode of operation, it brings low-cost photography to everyday folks and introduces the concept of the snapshot. The Brownie Camera is wildly popular (more than 100,000 are sold in the first year alone) and is a huge marketing success for Eastman Kodak.

1900 — The Feminization of Teaching as a Profession

While men use teaching positions as stepping stones to more lucrative jobs in government, law or business, women flock to teaching because it is one of the few professions open to them. Circa 1900, nearly 75 percent of America's teachers are women, though very few rise to the level of administrators. Urban female teachers earn low wages, have no pension benefits or job security. Married women are barred from the classroom. Rural teachers struggle with the same issues, along with the added burden of working in rundown schools that lack even the most basic resources. At this time, only 31 states require school attendance for children ages 8-14.

1900 — Frances Benjamin Johnston: Photojournalism Pioneer

Born into a wealthy and well-connected family, portrait photographer Frances Benjamin Johnston leverages her social status to gain access to many influential and famous subjects, including Susan B. Anthony, Mark Twain and Booker T. Washington. (Back in 1894, she opened her own studio in Washington D.C. and was the lone female photographer in town.) Johnston is a constant advocate for the role of women in the new art of photography. She sets tongues a-wagging when she takes a photographic "Self Portrait (as a New Woman)" in which she is smoking a cigarette with one hand and

clutching a fancy beer stein with the other. While portraiture is her strong suit, Johnston also photographs many gardens and buildings to encourage the preservation of historic structures.

1900 — Settlement Houses: The Dawn of Modern Social Work

By the turn of the century, there are more than 100 settlement houses in American cities, one of the first being Jane Addams and Ellen Gates Starr's Hull House in Chicago, which was founded in 1889. Settlements support European immigrants — few of whom speak English — by providing day care nurseries, kindergartens, mothers' clubs, art classes and educational programs. As the settlement movement evolves, funds are raised to build gymnasiums, auditoriums, communal dining facilities and living spaces. Hull House also breaks new ground by offering opportunities for young social workers to acquire professional training.

1900 — The Summer Olympics Welcomes the Ladies

Officially known as the Games of the II Olympiad, the international multi-sport event takes place in Paris, France, from May 14 through October 28, 1900. For the first time, women athletes are allowed to compete, and they do so in the areas of sailing, lawn tennis and golf. Unfortunately, the Games are poorly marketed and unorganized. This results in confusion over exactly who the first female Olympic gold medal winner is — although American golfer Margaret Abbott is among the contenders for that honor.

Above:
Johnston, Frances Benjamin, photographer. Frances Benjamin Johnston, full-length portrait, seated in front of fireplace, facing left, holding cigarette in one hand and a beer stein in the other, in her Washington, D.C. studio, 1896. Photograph. https://www.loc.gov/item/98502934/.

This Page:
Top: Professional group portrait. Inscribed "Glee Club, 1899" on back.

Bottom: Snapshot, mature women, rural Wisconsin, late 1890s or early 1900s.

1900 — "Sister Carrie" Is a Fabulous, Trampy Social Climber

Theodore Dreiser's first novel, "Sister Carrie," shocks American readers with its realistic portrayal of a young woman's determination to climb out of poverty. Her struggle causes her to be absolutely unladylike! When factory work proves too dreary, Carrie becomes a traveling salesman's arm candy. She then embarks on an affair with yet another man, and tags along when he embezzles company money and flees to Canada. The two eventually settle in New York, where Carrie is not punished for her misdeeds, but instead becomes a successful actress! "Sister Carrie" creates such a scandal after it is printed on November 8, 1900, that its publication is halted and the book is withdrawn from circulation.

1900 — Carrie Nation Does Not Have the Christmas Spirit

Prohibitionist and amateur hatchet-wielder Carrie Nation visits the bar (and smashes a giant mirror) at the Eaton Hotel in Wichita, Kansas, on December 27, 1900. Her vandalism ends up causing several thousand dollars' worth of damage and gets her tossed in jail. Having been married to an alcoholic, Nation has no tolerance for liquor or anyone who drinks it. She continues saloon-busting for several years and is arrested 13 more times before hitting the lecture circuit in support of temperance. Nation also sells souvenir hatchets on the side to finance her anti-booze efforts.

1901 — Alice Roosevelt: Dramatic White House Diva

Vice President Theodore Roosevelt assumes the office of President of the United States after the assassination of William McKinley in September 1901. As a result, his eldest daughter, Alice Roosevelt, becomes an instant celebrity and fashion icon. In an era defined by social conformity, Alice smokes cigarettes, flirts with men, goes out unchaperoned, parties late into the night, engages in voodoo and gambles. Alice's radical behavior causes her father to say, "I can either run the country or I can attend to Alice, but I cannot possibly do both."

1901 — Marconi Sends a Telegraph; Paves the Way for the Radio

Italian inventor Guglielmo Marconi sends the first trans-Atlantic telegraph message from Cornwall, England to Newfoundland, Canada, on December 12, 1901. (Serbian-American scientist Nikola Tesla had actually developed the technology in 1891.) Three years later, after receiving financial support from Andrew Carnegie and Thomas Edison, Marconi receives the U.S. Patent for the invention of the radio. (To this day, nobody is certain who invented the radio, but these were main players in the whole mess.)

Above and Below: Studio portraits, early 1900s.

1902 — The Vacuum Cleaner Makes Life a Little Less Filthy

The vacuum cleaner makes its formal debut as a go-to housekeeping device when it is used at Westminster Abbey to prepare for the coronation of King Edward VII on August 9, 1902. Inventor Hubert Cecil Booth's original model, patented the year before, had been a massive, horse-drawn unit that had to be parked outside a building, with long hoses fed through the windows during the vacuuming process. Within six years, technological advancements create portable vacuums (sold by the new Hoover Company) that make carpet cleaning a one-woman job.

1903 — The National Women's Trade Union League is Founded

In this organization, poor women, social reformers and wealthy donors from prominent families join together to improve wages and working conditions for females. The National Women's Trade Union League becomes a central meeting place for reform-minded gals of all walks of life. Its members fight to eliminate sweatshops and support the formation of labor unions.

1903 — Crayola Crayons: Imagine a Rainbow in a Box

Edwin Binney and his wife, Alice Stead Binney, a former schoolteacher, develop a new, non-toxic paraffin wax crayon and decide to name it the "Crayola." Alice coins the term by combining the French word *craie* (chalk) and *ola* (oily). The first boxes retail for five cents and contain eight crayons:

Above:
Studio portrait, early 1900s.

Below:
Studio portrait, early 1900s. Inscribed on the back "Unknown to me."

black, brown, blue, red, purple, orange, yellow and green. Edwin Binney markets Crayola Crayons with his partner C. Harold Smith and the lives of elementary school students are forever changed.

1903 — Mother Jones Organizes "The March of the Mill Children"

Labor organizer (and genius publicity queen) Mother Jones leads a caravan of women and striking children on a three-week trek from Philadelphia to New York City to advocate the end of child labor and horrible working conditions in factories. The group starts out on July 7, 1903. They reach New York City on July 23 and parade up Second Avenue by torchlight. Three days later, at Coney Island, Jones puts the children in animal cages to dramatize the inhumane treatment they receive at work. Jones extends the journey to make a public (and uninvited) stop at President's Theodore Roosevelt's Oyster Bay summer home on July 29.

1903 — That Window Contraption is Dangerous, Little Lady!

While riding on a streetcar during a visit to New York City, an Alabama tourist named Mary Anderson watches as the driver disembarks time and again to clean off his snow-covered windshield. Inspiration strikes. While still on the streetcar, Anderson begins to draw sketches of a wiper device. She envisions spring-loaded blades that could be activated with a lever near the steering wheel. The sweeping motion of these blades could keep windows free of debris, snow or rain! On November 10, 1903, Anderson receives a 17-year patent for her invention. She tries to market it, but companies scoff at her idea, saying that windshield wipers will distract drivers and cause accidents. Anderson's patent expires before she can convince anyone to use her invention and she never sees a dime of profit.

1903 — Here Comes the Airplane!

Air travel becomes a reality when Orville and Wilbur Wright make the first successful powered airplane flight on December 17, 1903 over the sand dunes at Kitty Hawk, North Carolina. Orville pilots the propeller-driven biplane on the inaugural flight, which covers 120 feet and lasts just 12 seconds. As they experiment and become more comfortable with the plane's capabilities, Wilbur is at the controls for the day's fourth and final flight (the longest), which lasts 59 seconds and travels 852 feet. Since the Wright brothers are experienced amateur photographers, they also set a camera up on a tripod to capture their historic first flight on film.

1903 — The Iroquois Theater Fire in Chicago, Illinois

Tragedy strikes in the Windy City on December 30, 1903 when a fire breaks out in the new Renaissance-style Iroquois Theater on Randolph Street.

Nearly 2,000 people — many of them women and children on holiday break from school — had gathered for a matinee performance by the popular musical comedian Eddie Foy. Blocked exits and the lack of emergency lighting, sprinkler systems or a fire-safety plan lead to the deaths of more than 600 people. In the aftermath, more building-code violations are found.

Above:
Professional group portrait, 1900s.

Below:
Studio portrait, early 1900s.

1904 — Ida Tarbell Takes Aim at Standard Oil

Muckraking writer Ida Tarbell unleashes her groundbreaking two-volume work, "The History of the Standard Oil Company" in 1904. It is a collection of articles Tarbell had previously written for *McClure's Magazine*. The book features detailed research and interviews with sources inside tycoon John D. Rockefeller's monopoly. Tarbell's methods become the gold standard in the nascent field of investigative journalism and her reporting contributes to the eventual breakup of Standard Oil under the Sherman Antitrust Act.

1904 — The New York City Subway Begins Operation

Overcrowding, vermin-infested tenements and rampant disease make New York City a tough place to live at the beginning of the 20th century. Commuting by horse-drawn conveyance is no picnic, either. All things considered, it's no surprise that on October 27, 1904, more than 100,000

people pay a nickel fare to ride the subway through the city for the first time. The 9.1-mile-long subterranean line features 28 stations between City Hall in lower Manhattan to 145th Street and Broadway in Harlem.

1905 — Madam C.J. Walker Revolutionizes the Beauty Industry

Using a formula that came to her in a dream, Madam C. J. Walker (born Sarah Breedlove on a Louisiana plantation in 1867 to emancipated slaves) creates a line of hair-care products for African-American women. Walker then promotes her products by traveling around the country to offer live demonstrations. Her determination and business savvy pay off when she becomes one of the first self-made female millionaires in the United States. Walker embraces philanthropy and uses her vast wealth to support educational, social and political causes that benefit African-Americans.

1905 — Song, Dance and Cinema — All for a Nickel!

In Pittsburgh, Pennsylvania, more than 400 people line up to attend the grand opening of the world's first nickelodeon on June 19, 1905. The storefront theater — which has opera seating for 96 patrons and standing room for everyone else — offers a mix of live vaudeville acts and short films. Tickets go for five cents, giving the new type of entertainment venue its name. Nickelodeons continue to show films until Hollywood motion pictures become recognized as an up-and-coming art form and larger, more opulent theaters are built to screen them.

1906 — The Great Earthquake Hits San Francisco

In the early morning hours of April 18, 1906, an earthquake measuring 7.9 on the Richter scale strikes the northern coast of California, near San Francisco. The tremors are felt from Los Angeles to Oregon. Though the earthquake lasts just 60 seconds, it sets off fires that burn for three days. The water supply, which is crippled by the earthquake, has to be shut off, leaving no way to fight the fires. The damage in San Francisco is cataclysmic and the entire central business district is destroyed. Approximately 3,000 people are killed and half the city is left homeless. Chaos and looting ensue.

1906 — Congress Passes the Pure Food Act

A key piece of Progressive Era legislation, the Pure Food and Drug Act prohibits the sale or transportation of adulterated, misbranded, poisonous or deleterious food, drugs, medicines and liquor. President Theodore Roosevelt signs the act, along with the Federal Meat Inspection Act, which ensures that meat would be slaughtered and processed under sanitary conditions. (The 1906 publication of Upton Sinclair's novel, "The Jungle," which makes everyone want to hurl, motivates these reforms.)

This Page:
Top: Snapshot, ladies in "cartwheel" style hats, outdoors with young children, 1900s.

Bottom: Snapshot, woman posing with a tennis racket, 1900s. (Note: Calf-length, short-sleeved attire for female tennis players did not appear until after World War I.)

Opposite Page:
Studio portrait, 1900s.

Above:
Outdoor informal portrait, 1900s.

Below:
Studio portrait, early 1900s.

1908 — The Electric Washing Machine Sets Women Free at Last

While earlier devices were used to lessen the drudgery of wash day, it isn't until running water, the electric heater and the electric motor are combined that the revolution truly begins. Introduced by the Hurley Machine Company of Chicago, The Thor debuts as the first electric-powered washing machine. Since The Thor uses an electric motor to turn clothes through the water, and doesn't require a hand-crank or steam power, women do not need to be present during the wash cycle. The end result is spare time!

1908 — The All-New 10-Hour Work Day for Women

In the case of *Muller v. Oregon*, the U.S. Supreme Court upholds the right of states to pass protective legislation for female workers. At this time, it's common for American women to endure unsafe working conditions and do so for long hours with low wages. While the win in court limits the work day to 10 hours and protects the health of female employees, it also reaffirms the belief that women were weak, second-class workers. The court rules that women have "always been dependent on men" and that "in a struggle for subsistence she is not an equal competitor with her brother."

1908 — Home Economics Becomes Legit

Brainy engineer and chemist Ellen H. Swallow Richard, the first woman to be admitted to the Massachusetts Institute of Technology, graduates in 1873 and becomes its first female instructor. Richard, an early "ecofeminist," is the first to integrate chemistry with the study of nutrition. Her work of applying innovations in science and technology to homemaking tasks results in the founding of the American Home Economics Association in 1908.

1908 — The Model T Rolls Off the Assembly Line

Mass production methods make it possible for the Ford Motor Company to introduce the Ford Model T on October 1, 1908. While this new vehicle retails for $850, nearly one-third of the price of other vehicles on the market, it is still beyond the reach of many Americans — including the workers who build them in Detroit, Michigan. Ford increases assembly line efficiency and reduces the car's price over the next few years, eventually selling the Model T to millions of consumers and making travel accessible to an emerging American middle class. Though "motoring" in open cars on dusty, unpaved roads is perceived as a masculine activity, an increasing number of women get behind the wheel. The Model T becomes an avenue for female independence outside the realm of the family home.

1908 — National Association of Colored Graduate Nurses

In an effort to circumvent the segregation they encounter in their profession, 52 African-American nurses meet in New York City in 1908 to found the National Association of Colored Graduate Nurses. Martha Minerva Franklin, who organizes the gathering after two years of research and a direct-mail campaign, is elected as the organization's first president. The NACGN plans to eradicate discrimination in the nursing profession, bolster the leadership of African-American nurses and advance standards in the field. The NACGN holds its first convention in Boston in 1909.

1908 — Times Square Gets Lit on New Year's Eve

On December 31, 1907, *The New York Times* publishes a story that advises its readers to "Watch the Times Tower: The Descent of an Electric Ball Will Mark the Arrival of 1908 To-night." Positioned atop a flagpole on the building's roof, the ball is five feet in diameter and features 216 internal electric lamps. The newspaper had originally planned a fireworks display, but when the city of New York prohibits it, a new tradition is born.

1909 — International Women's Day: Girl Power Goes Global

After thousands of Jewish garment workers strike in protest of conditions in New York's shirtwaist factories, the Socialist Party of America celebrates the first National Women's Day on February 28, 1909. Galvanized by progressive reformers and organizers, females turn up the volume on their demands for shorter hours, better pay and voting rights. In 1910, the day receives international recognition as a time to honor women's rights and activism.

Above:
Snapshot, taken on balcony, dated 1907.

Below:
Studio portrait, 1900s.

1909 — The NAACP: Fighting for Racial Equality

Following a deadly 1908 race riot in Springfield — the capital of Illinois and home town of President Abraham Lincoln — the National Association for the Advancement of Colored People is formed. A group of 60 people are present for the founding, seven of whom are African-American, including W. E. B. Du Bois, Ida B. Wells-Barnett and Mary Church Terrell. The NAACP intends to secure for all people the equal protection of rights guaranteed in the Constitution and to eliminate race-based discrimination.

1909 — The First Coast-to-Coast All-Girl Road Trip

Housewife and part-time endurance driver Alice Ramsey, age 21, accepts a challenge from the Maxwell-Briscoe Company to drive one of their touring cars across the United States. The company hopes the publicity stunt will illustrate the safety and reliability of their vehicles. (There are only about 130,000 cars in the entire country at this time.) Leaving New York City on June 9, along with her two sister-in-laws and a female friend, Ramsey copes with horrible road conditions, flooding streams, flat tires and mechanical failures. She motors into San Francisco on August 7, 1909 — having made the journey in just 59 days.

This Page:
Top: Group snapshot. Inscribed on back "Wedding Party Cake, 1906."

Bottom: Studio portrait, Baltimore, Maryland, mid-1900s.

Opposite Page:
Studio portrait, late 1900s or early 1910s.

Fashion Footnotes from Photos of the 1900s

The 1900s — "The Edwardian Era"

The Edwardian era covers the reign of Britain's King Edward VII, from 1901 to 1910. Marked by elegance and luxury among the upper classes in both England and America, it is also defined by social protests and shifting traditions. The Edwardian Era and the global economic dominance of the British Empire come to an end after World War I.

Fashion trends from the decade include:

- The Wasp Waist (Created by an extremely tight corset)
- The Hourglass Figure (Ample womanly bosom and large curvy hips)
- "Cottage Loaf" Hair Style (Very long hair, pinned up, piled high and multi-tiered, like a loaf of fresh bread)
- Ladies' Style Icon: The Gibson Girl (An unrealistic cartoon goddess with an air of upper-class superiority; the brainchild of illustrator Charles Dana Gibson)
- Dominant Fashion Idea #1: Large, elaborate "Cartwheel Hat;" decorated with feathers, flowers, lace, bows, fruit, fake birds. These huge, showy hats could weigh up to 50 pounds.
- Dominant Fashion Idea #2: Long, much-adorned skirt; cinched waist; more bows, lace, ruffles and flowers
- Dominant Fashion Idea #3: The more stuff you had on you, the more fashionable you were. A fussy parasol and gloves were cool, also.
- Dominant aesthetic of the day: Art Nouveau (Organic, curvilinear, Celtic influence; celebration of nature)
- By 1907-1908, style evolves from the Hourglass Corset to the Safety Corset. The S-shaped Safety Corset creates the "Pigeon Breast" shape. A gal's butt and chest stick out to make curvy silhouette.
- Wealthy women wear dusters and veils for "motoring" in their cars.
- The Shirtwaist is everywhere. It is always white, ivory or cream. A woman's skirt matches her jacket. These pieces represent the start of "ladies' separates" as we know them today.

Above:
Studio portraits featuring the wide-brimmed "Cartwheel Hat" (top) and the "Pigeon Breast" bodice (bottom), 1900s.

Opposite Page:
Professional outdoor portrait, 1900s.
(An example of "Gibson Girl" style)

1910s: World War I, Social Protests and the Spanish Flu Pandemic

"America's future will be determined by the home and the school. The child becomes largely what he is taught; hence we must watch what we teach, and how we live."

—*Jane Addams (1860-1935), American social worker, activist and founder of Hull House*

In the early 1910s, it is widely accepted that a woman's place is in the home, school or church. However, World War I quickly changes that paradigm, as the ladies are presented with new opportunities for social interaction and volunteerism that yield previously unimagined levels of female independence.

During the war, jobs that had been considered inappropriate for anyone with a uterus are now fair game. By some estimates, more than 20,000 women work overseas as nurses and medical aides, while others serve as ambulance drivers or telephone and radio operators. In the United States, the lack of menfolk means that females are hired to work in places like munitions factories — although they do so for lower wages than male employees would earn. These jobs (far different than domestic service positions with wealthy, genteel families) allow the ladies to develop identities outside of the scope of the patriarchal home.

Farms are giving way to factories, many of which employ children, women or recent immigrants. Desperate to escape life in the Jim Crow South, nearly a million African-Americans head north in search of personal safety and better wages. The overcrowded American cities, home to hundreds of thousands of poverty-stricken families, are incubators for disease, vice and crime. In order to combat these problems, new social movements are born.

By 1910, Germans are the largest non-English speaking immigrant group in America. However, as the war escalates, patriotism swells and anti-German sentiment takes root. Government propaganda posters depict the defeat of "The Huns" and encourage the purchase of Liberty Bonds as a means of supporting the nation and the military.

She might seem demure in her long, tailored skirt and ostrich-plumed hat, but the American woman has an iron will. Above all, she knows that without a vote, without a political voice, she can't whip our country into shape. And she's ready to do just that — until the dreaded Spanish Flu rears its ugly head.

This Page:
Above: Studio portrait, early 1910s.
Below: Arcade portrait, 1910s.

Previous Spread:
Left: Snapshot, group photo, inscribed on back "Decoration Day, 1919."
Right: Studio portrait, 1910s.

1910 — Beauty Is Only a Spa Visit Away

Elizabeth Arden (born Florence Nightingale Graham in 1884 in rural Canada) reinvents herself when she opens her first Red Door Salon in 1910 on Fifth Avenue in New York City. Arden wants to help other ladies find their own inner divas as well. Her guiding philosophy is that being beautiful is every woman's birthright. Furthermore, she views makeup as a subtle and scientific tool that can enhance one's God-given assets. Arden decides that her salon's front door should be a bold shade of red, not only for visual marketing purposes, but as a symbol of female independence.

1911 — The Triangle Shirtwaist Factory Fire

Working conditions in most factories are abysmal at the beginning of the 20th century, with long hours and low pay being the norm. On March 25, 1911, a fire in the Triangle Shirtwaist Company's factory in New York City claims the lives of 146 female workers, the majority of whom are Italian and Jewish immigrants in their teens and early 20s. Trapped behind locked exit doors, the women are forced to jump to the street 10 stories below in their attempt to escape the burning building. The disaster leads to improved factory safety standards and better working conditions.

1912 — Anita Loos: Motion Picture Mastermind

Former child stage actress and freelance writer Anita Loos hits the big time when director D.W. Griffith hires her in 1912 as the first-ever staff screenwriter at the Triangle Film Corporation. For a salary of $75 a week, Loos creates film scripts for some of Hollywood's biggest stars including Douglas Fairbanks, Mary Pickford and the Gish Sisters. (Historical footnote: Loos is never accused of sexual harassment.)

1912 — Girl Scouts Hold First Troop Meeting

In the middle of the Progressive Era, at a time when women can't vote, Juliette Gordon Low launches an organization to inspire girls to excel. Low had lived in England with her first husband for many years and had been a Girl Guide leader during that time. After returning to her hometown of Savannah, Georgia, Low gathers 18 girls together on March 12, 1912 and creates the first troop of American Girl Guides. Low's program offers educational and outdoor opportunities designed to enrich the girls' lives. The name is changed to the Girl Scouts of America the following year.

1912 — The RMS Titanic Disaster

Described as the world's most luxurious floating hotel, the buzz is considerable when the RMS Titanic sets sail on its maiden voyage from Southampton to New York. Five days into the journey on April 15, 1912,

the Titanic hits an iceberg in the Atlantic Ocean that takes a big chunk out of her starboard side. There are not enough lifeboats and the water is frigid — cold enough to incapacitate many passengers who jump overboard. After two hours and 40 minutes of pandemonium, the Titanic sinks. Of the more than 2,200 passengers and crew on board, more than 1,500 perish.

1912 — The Gish Sisters Give "The Flickers" a Try

After a decade of stage work, Lillian Gish takes on her first silent movie role in D.W. Griffith's "An Unseen Enemy." She appears along with her sister, Dorothy, in the 17-minute film, which is released on September 9, 1912. The plot tells the unfortunate tale of two young girls who are held at gunpoint by their own housekeeper — a woman who wants to rob them of the proceeds from their late father's estate. Lillian goes on to make more than two dozen movies over the next two years, and becomes a trailblazing actress in the rapidly developing Hollywood film industry.

1912 — A New Development in Midtown

New York's Grand Central Terminal opens for business in February 1913 and becomes a transportation hub for the entire metropolitan area. A blend of beauty and functionality, it features a main concourse with 125-foot vaulted ceilings, as well as separate levels for subway, pedestrian and automobile traffic. Its truly grand design includes bronze and stone carvings, ornamental inscriptions, decorative flourishes, and sculpted oak leaves and acorns. By burying the railroad tracks underground, developers are able to lease the space above ground to help fund the terminal's construction.

Above:
Portrait with back inscription "J. Ringle, Augusta Frey Ringle, Marie Ringle and people they met on the ship going to Europe in 1914 (June 7th)."

Below:
Snapshot, woman on sidewalk, 1910s.

Above:
Dale, Benjamin M., -1951, Artist, and U.S. Records League Of Women Voters. Official program - Woman suffrage procession, Washington, D.C. March 3, 1913. Photograph. https://www.loc.gov/item/94507639/.

Instead of being a common rail yard, Grand Central is the catalyst that brings expensive offices, hotels, restaurants, shops, and fashionable homes to the neighborhood.

1912 — Children's Bureau Is Established

Responding to pressure from social reformers, President William Howard Taft and the federal government create the United States Children's Bureau in 1912. The original goal for the bureau is to investigate the relationship between poverty and infant mortality. Its mission soon expands to include prenatal care, disease prevention, and the protection of child laborers.

1913 — Woman Suffrage Procession: It's Alice Paul, Y'All!

Women's rights activist Alice Paul organizes the first suffrage parade in Washington, D.C. on March 3, 1913, the day before Woodrow Wilson's inauguration. Thousands of angry ladies march down Pennsylvania Avenue along with bands, floats and mounted brigades to protest "the present political organization of society, from which women are excluded." In other words, they want the right to vote! Marchers are tripped and assaulted by spectators, many of whom are men in town for the presidential inauguration. Police do not intervene (many of them disapprove of the suffragists) and 100 marchers are hospitalized by the day's end.

1913 — That's Puzzling ... But It Does Help Pass the Time

Voracious readers and lovers of language discover a newfangled way to amuse themselves when the very first crossword puzzle is published in the *New York World*. The user-friendly word game, is shaped like a diamond, has no internal black squares and offers mind-bending clues such as "What bargain hunters enjoy." (The answer: Sales.)

1913 — Elizabeth Gurley Flynn Organizes the Patterson Strike

Wages are low. The hours are long. Working conditions are abysmal. Fed up with their jobs in the textile industry, nearly 25,000 silk workers strike and shut down hundreds of silk mills and dye houses in Paterson, New Jersey. One of the strike's most visible organizers, feminist leader Elizabeth Gurley Flynn, advocates for the rights of women and child workers and manages to unite strikers across racial boundaries. The strike begins in February and runs through July of 1913. It gains attention not only for its duration, but for the number and prominence of its supporters.

1913 — Susan LaFlesche, Frontier Physician and Working Mom

After graduating from Woman's Medical College of Pennsylvania in 1889, Susan LaFlesche becomes the first female Native American doctor. While settling on the East Coast would have afforded her a lush life, LaFlesche returns to her childhood home on the Omaha Indian Reservation in northeast Nebraska. She labors tirelessly, caring for more than 1,200 people who suffer from ailments that include malnutrition, diphtheria and influenza. In between making house calls in a horse-drawn buggy and treating patients in her own home, LaFlesche marries Henry Picotte, a Sioux from South Dakota, and has two sons. When her husband dies from the effects of tuberculosis and alcoholism, she joins the temperance movement and maintains her medical practice while raising her young boys. In 1913, Dr. LaFlesche opens a hospital on reservation land near Walthill, Nebraska. The hospital is built without government financing and is open to anyone who is ill, regardless of age, sex or ethnicity.

1913 — The Ford Assembly Line Starts Moving

On December 1, the continuous-flow production methods used in flour mills, breweries, canneries and industrial bakeries are adopted at the Ford Motor Company's new plant in Highland Park, Michigan. Assembly line mass production reduces the time it takes to build a car from more than 12 hours to less than three. This development also slashes the price of a Ford Model T so that more Americans — including the factory workers themselves — can afford to own one. (In 1912, Ford produces 82,388 Model

This Spread:
Above: Snapshot, fashionable lady, 1910s.
Below: Snapshot, girl in hammock, 1913.
Opposite Page: Snapshot, woman posing with car decorated for parade, 1910s.

Above:
Snapshot, inscribed on front "Aunt Agnes & Jeanne," 1910s.

Below:
Studio portrait, inscribed on front and again on back with "Rollie, 1914."

Ts and the touring car sells for about $600. By 1916, the combination of large-scale production and competitive wages for factory employees help increase Model T production to 585,388 and drops the sticker price to $360.)

1914 — I Remember Mama and Yo Mama, Too, for That Matter

The second Sunday in May becomes "Mother's Day" in 1914 when President Woodrow Wilson designates it as an official U.S. holiday. Anna Jarvis, who organized the first Mother's Day celebration at her church in Grafton, West Virginia in 1908, envisions it as a means of honoring her own deceased mother. Jarvis becomes increasingly disgusted as Mother's Day evolves into a robust revenue stream for florists, stationers and candy companies and spends the rest of her life fighting its commercialization.

1914 — I Think We Could Make Better Time If We Go This Way ...

Completed with a jaw-dropping price tag of $350 million, the Panama Canal officially opens on August 15, 1914. The lock-type canal is essentially a 51-mile waterway that connects the Atlantic and Pacific Oceans through the Isthmus of Panama. The Panama Canal allows ships to travel between the east and west coasts of the United States without having to sail south and circle all the way around Cape Horn in South America — a short cut of about 8,000 nautical miles. The 10-year project requires the construction of the largest earth dam and the biggest moving gates the world has ever known. (The cargo ship SS Ancon makes first official canal crossing.)

1914 — The Brassiere Is Patented in the United States

On November 3, 1914, New York socialite Mary Phelps Jacob receives U.S. Patent Number 1,115,674 for a revolutionary new undergarment that she calls the "Backless Brassiere." Jacobs, who is annoyed with corsets that peek out from underneath some of her more daring evening gowns, creates the prototype herself, with a little assistance from her French maid. She designs it by standing in front of a mirror and constructing the brassiere out of two pocket handkerchiefs, a handful of ribbons and some pins. Boobs everywhere are grateful for Jacobs' support and all-American ingenuity. While the "Backless Brassiere" is initially well-received by female consumers, it becomes wildly popular during World War I, when the government asks women to stop buying corsets in order to conserve metal.

1915 — One Ringy Dingy! Long Distance Calling!

On January 25, 1915, Alexander Graham Bell, stationed in New York City, rings up his former assistant Thomas Augustus Watson in San Francisco, and repeats his famous statement, "Mr. Watson, come here. I want you." The phone call is the official initiation for AT&T's transcontinental phone

service. President Woodrow Wilson and the mayors of both cities are also involved in the call, which is placed in conjunction with celebrations surrounding the Panama-Pacific International Exposition.

Above:
Bain News Service, Publisher. 14-year-old striker, Fola La Follette and Rose Livingston, Photograph. 1913. https://www.loc.gov/item/2014692415/.

1915 — Catt's Back, This Time with a Big Pile of Money

After the death of her husband, Carrie Chapman Catt returns for a second term as president of the National Woman Suffrage Association (NAWSA). Catt understands the need for a devoted team and an active communications network. Using the proceeds from her late husband's estate, along with the $1 million that Mrs. Frank Leslie had willed to her to use for women's suffrage, Catt creates a centralized, tiered organization. It operates with military precision and is fueled by righteous female indignation.

Below:
Studio portrait, 1910s.

1915 — The RMS Lusitania Is Sunk By Torpedo

The British ocean liner RMS Lusitania is torpedoed by a German U-boat on May 7, 1915, while en route from New York to Liverpool, England. The crew attempts to start evacuation efforts, but only six out of 48 lifeboats launch successfully, while others break apart completely. Within 20 minutes, the Lusitania sinks and nearly 1,200 people drown, including 128 American citizens. The event turns public opinion against Germany, even though the United States will not enter World War I for two more years.

1915 — The Woman's Peace Party Is Founded

In response to the war in Europe, which had begun the previous year, several notable women, including Jane Addams, Charlotte Perkins Gilman,

Above:
Studio portrait, 1910s.

Below:
Snapshot, outdoor group photo, 1910s.

Opposite Page:
Studio portrait, image printed with decorative oval mat, 1910s

Alice Hamilton, Florence Kelley, Edith Green Balch and Carrie Chapman Catt found the Woman's Peace Party (WPP). They begin organizing public demonstrations to formally protest World War I.

1915 — Suffragettes Make a Scene on Fifth Avenue

By bringing together women of various social and economic backgrounds, the suffrage parade becomes a very effective tool in the fight for women's rights. Media coverage, whether positive or negative, also helps publicize the cause. Though smaller parades had taken place with increasing frequency during the previous decade, it's the big turnout in New York City that really kicks female advocacy into high gear. On October 23, 1915, Dr. Anna Howard Shaw and Carrie Chapman Catt, founder of the League of Women Voters, lead an estimated 25,000 women in a suffrage parade in Manhattan. Many participants are clad in flowing, white dresses. The multigenerational crowd, which stretches three miles long, protests for the right to vote. This high-profile event illustrates the magnitude of the women's rights movement — which had begun back in 1848, when the Seneca Falls Convention passed the first resolution in favor of women's suffrage.

1916 — Jeannette Rankin: The First Woman in the U.S. Congress

Jeannette Rankin, a suffragist and schoolteacher, runs for a congressional seat in her home state of Montana two years after women in that state are enfranchised. In November 1916, Rankin becomes the first woman elected to the U.S. House of Representatives. A lifelong pacifist, she is the only member of Congress to formally oppose America's participation in both World War I and World War II.

1916 — The NPS: Keeping It Green and Clean for Us All

The National Park Service is created on August 25, 1916 when President Woodrow Wilson signs a piece of legislation informally known as "The Organic Act." Previously part of the Department of the Interior, the NPS becomes a new federal bureau that will protect the country's national parks, monuments and reservations. Its mission is to "conserve the scenery and the natural and historic objects and the wildlife" in America's 35 existing parks, as well as those yet to be established. The NPS is responsible with preserving and protecting these sites for "the enjoyment of future generations."

1916 — The Work of Georgia O'Keefe Is Showcased in NYC

Photographer and modern art sponsor Alfred Stieglitz exhibits a group of charcoal drawings by Georgia O'Keefe at his prestigious "291" gallery on Fifth Avenue in New York City. As a result, O'Keefe then earns her own

Above:
Snapshot, woman in the snow, 1910s.

Below:
Studio portrait, inscribed on front in ink "Heaps of Love to my own Little Eleanor," 1910s.

one-woman show at the gallery in 1917. O'Keefe quits her teaching job the following year and moves to New York to begin her full-time career as an artist. Her focus on abstract forms — in both urban and rural environments — eventually makes her a major figure in American art.

1916 — The "Birth Control Sisters" Get Busted in Brooklyn

In October 1916, Margaret Sanger and her sister, Ethel Byrne, open a birth control clinic in the Brownsville section of Brooklyn, New York — the first clinic of its kind in the United States. After just 10 days, authorities close down the clinic for violating the Comstock Law of 1873 and arrest Sanger and her sister. The Comstock Law not only thwarted efforts to protect mothers from excessive childbearing and children from being born sick, weak, unwanted and unprovided for, but was responsible, directly or indirectly, for the deaths of a million women during the 60 years in which it was enforced. These deaths occurred among mothers who were the victims of abortions or of bearing children when in poor physical health.

1917 — The United States Enters World War I

Having won his second term in office in 1916 with the slogan "America First," President Woodrow Wilson favors neutrality. Things change in March 1917 when German submarines sink three U.S. merchant ships. Backed by his Cabinet and the newspapers, Wilson calls for Congress to meet and war on Germany is declared on April 6, 1917. (After the sinking of the passenger liner RMS Lusitania in 1915, anti-German sentiment already exists.)

1917 — Isadora Duncan: A Very Different Kind of Twirl

Breaking from rigid ballet technique, modern dance diva Isadora Duncan pioneers an organic style of movement that blends folk dance, natural energy and athleticism. Duncan dances barefoot (a rebellious act in itself) and often wears a flowing Greek tunic. This ensemble showcases her sturdy physique, and occasionally, a nude thigh or breast. In 1917, after returning from South America, Duncan launches her only successful American tour with a series of performances at the New York Metropolitan Opera House.

1917 — The Riot in East St. Louis, Illinois

Racial tension had been escalating for years in East St. Louis, the result of thousands of black workers relocating from the South in search of war-related factory jobs. In April of 1917, the white employees of the Aluminum Ore Company go on strike. Hundreds of black workers are hired to replace them. By May 28, angry whites lodge formal complaints with the city council against the black migrants. When word of an attempted robbery of a white man by an armed black man spreads through the city, mob mentality takes over. On July 2, whites begin randomly attacking any African-Americans they find — men, women and children are beaten, shot and terrorized in their own homes. Some are dragged from streetcars and lynched while police officers and state militiamen do not intervene. In the aftermath of the riot, the official death toll is said to be 40 blacks and eight whites, but the numbers cannot be verified because local investigations are inept.

1917 — "The Hello Girls" Come to the Rescue

When it becomes apparent that U.S. soldiers on the Western front can't handle the telecommunications piece of fighting on foreign soil, General John Pershing calls for backup. At his urgent request, the Signal Corps Female Telephone Operators Unit is formed. These lady "wire experts" have to be bilingual in English and French. Over 7,000 women apply, but only 450 pass the rigorous background checks and psychological testing. Of those who qualify for special training, 223 are actually sent abroad. Many of these ladies are former switchboard operators or telecommunications company employees. In their new roles, they quickly become known as "The Hello Girls." Each Signal Corps operator recruit has to shell out $300 to $500 for her uniform: a dark blue wool Norfolk jacket and matching long skirt, black high-top shoes and brown Army boots, hat, overcoat, rubber raincoat, woolen underwear and black sateen bloomers. (The latter are required for modesty's sake, in case the wind ever blows her skirt up.)

1917 — Alice Paul Leads NWP's Protests at the White House

After Woodrow Wilson's re-election, Alice Paul calls for the National Woman's Party to picket the White House. Paul wants to convince the president to generate Congressional support for a constitutional suffrage amendment. After months of protests, the police announce that NWP members will receive jail time if they continue the effort. Between June and November 1917, Paul and 96 other suffragists are arrested and jailed for "obstructing traffic." When they go on a hunger strike to protest their arrests and treatment as political prisoners, they are tortured and force-fed.

1917 — Salvation Army Girls Fry Up a Little Bit of Heaven

Ensign Helen Purviance, a young, newly commissioned "Salvationist" from Indiana is working in a rain-soaked, dripping tent in France. She is teamed with her Salvation Army "Slum Sister," Ensign Margaret Sheldon, who had worked in Chicago with unwed mothers before the war. In September 1917, they decide to whip up something more nutritious than hot cocoa and fudge for the troops of the First Division ammunition train. Purviance and Sheldon scour the commissary and find flour, lard, sugar, baking powder, vanilla and condensed milk. They consider making pancakes, but have no

Above:
Studio portrait, 1910s.

Below:
Snapshot, inscribed on front in ink, "M. Nominigan. 1917. Little Katie."

Above:
Studio portrait, 1910s.

Below:
Snapshot, nurse wearing face mask, folding woolen blanket outdoors, 1910s.

plates, butter or molasses. Instead, they roll out the dough and cut it with a wine bottle to make crullers. They fry batches of seven in a small pan over a tiny, potbellied stove. On the first day, they serve 150 soldiers, earning Salvation Army ladies the permanent nickname of the "Doughnut Girls."

1917 — Prosthetics for Wounded Soldiers

Anna Coleman Ladd, who has traveled to France with her husband, a physician who oversees with the Red Cross Children's Bureau, becomes interested in the treatment of facially disfigured war veterans. A well-known sculptor in the United States, Mrs. Ladd sets up the American Red Cross "Studio for Portrait Masks" in Paris. Under her guidance, soldiers with mutilated faces are fitted for lifelike prosthetic masks that will replicate their original features and help them transition back into life at home.

1918 — The Emergence of Physical Therapy

Mary McMillan, an American physiotherapist who had trained in England, becomes one of the guiding forces behind the reconstruction profession. Under her leadership, two types of Army Medical Department "reconstruction aides" emerge. Physiotherapists provide massage, electro/hydro treatment and other therapeutic techniques. Occupational Therapists work with injured soldiers on rehabilitative activities such as crocheting, basketry, weaving, reading, writing, math, typing and mechanical drawing. Beyond these job descriptions, there is little that defines the occupation. "Reconstruction is a new word for a new work," Mary McMillan explains.

"The profession was born in response to a brand new need." McMillan goes on to become the founder of physical therapy in the United States.

1918 — U.S. Post Office's Airmail Service Takes Flight

Utilizing the relatively new mode of airplane transportation, in May of 1918, the United States Post Office begins regular airmail service between New York, Philadelphia and Washington, D.C. The early mail planes have no reliable instruments, radios, or other navigational aids. Pilots cover their routes by using landmarks and dead reckoning. Forced landings occur frequently due to bad weather, but fatalities are rare, since the planes are small, easy to maneuver and land at slow speeds. For this new service, Congress authorizes airmail postage of 24 cents per ounce.

1918 — Margaret Sanger Wins in the New York Court of Appeals

Two years after opening a birth control clinic in Brooklyn (and being arrested for doing so), Margaret Sanger wins her suit in New York to allow doctors to advise their married patients about birth control. Sanger argues that the 1873 Comstock Act violates the Constitution by jeopardizing women's physical well-being. She believes that in order for women to achieve equality in society and have healthier lives, they need to be able to choose when they want to bear children.

1918 — The Spanish Flu Pandemic Hits the United States

In September 1918, soldiers at an Army base near Boston begin dying from a mysterious illness. Details about the severity of the disease are kept quiet, as U.S. officials are concerned about bolstering public morale during the war. (Earlier cases had surfaced at Fort Riley, Kansas, in the spring of 1918.) The virus quickly spreads across the country, overfilling hospitals and necessitating the use of temporary morgues and mass graves in metropolitan areas. The U.S. also experiences a severe nursing shortage; many medical professionals have already been deployed to military camps. Ultimately, more than 675,000 Americans die from the Spanish Flu.

According to the Centers for Disease Control and Prevention:

It is estimated that about 500 million people, or one-third of the world's population, became infected with the influenza virus, and the number of deaths was believed to be at least 50 million worldwide. The pandemic was so severe that from 1917 to 1918, life expectancy in the United States fell by about 12 years, to 36.6 years for men and 42.2 years for women. There were high death rates in previously healthy people, including those between the ages of 20 and 40 years old, which was unusual because flu typically hits the very young and the very old more than young adults.

Above:
Studio portrait, 1910s.

Below:
Snapshot, sweeping the balcony, 1910s.

Above:
Snapshot, 1910s. This image shows an older woman wearing an outfit that dates to the late 1890s, while the young woman and the girl are dressed in beach attire that dates to the 1910s. Was Mother too proper to wear a "modern" bathing outfit? The answer is unclear. However, it's certain that her black frock-and-bonnet combo was easily the hottest, sweatiest ensemble on the beach that day. Hello, heatstroke!

Opposite Page:
Top: Snapshot, thoroughly modern women dressed in their finery, 1910s.

Bottom: Snapshot, woman picking wildflowers in a field, 1910s. Portable consumer cameras made these types of photographs increasingly common. Nature-themed images also reflected the American public's growing appreciation for conservation and unspoiled pastoral settings in the face of rapid advancements in modern technology and industry.

1919 — You Can Dial Me Directly!

The Western Electric model of the rotary dial telephone becomes popular in the United States in 1919. It uses a signaling technology called "pulse dialing." To place a call, the user must rotate each digit in numerical sequence on the phone's circular wheel. At the "finger stop" position, the dial is released and an electrical current generates pulses that decode each digit. The rotary phone is the first device that allows callers to connect their telephones to other parties without the aid of an operator.

1919 — Mary Pickford Co-Founds United Artists

When Mary Pickford, the actress known as "America's Sweetheart" and "The Girl with the Curls," signs a $1 million contract in 1916, she is just 24 years old. Though Pickford plays sweet little gals onscreen, her real-life business savvy makes her a guiding force in the burgeoning motion picture industry — and she has big ideas. Three years later, on February 5, 1919, Pickford teams up with D.W. Griffith, Charlie Chaplin and Douglas Fairbanks, Sr. to found the United Artists independent film production company.

1919 — The Grand Canyon: There's No Improving on Perfection

Private development of that ginormous hole in the ground in Arizona is outlawed on February 26, 1919, when President Woodrow Wilson signs the Grand Canyon National Park Act. Though it had already been declared a national monument in 1908 by the avid outdoorsman Theodore Roosevelt when he resided in the White House, the act officially ensures that this environmental treasure of the American West will remain pristine.

1919 — Democratic Evolution: Women and the Vote

What a long, strange trip it's been. On June 4, 1919, Congress, by joint resolution, approves the Women's Suffrage Amendment and sends it to the states for ratification. The amendment decrees that: *"The right of citizens of the United States to vote shall not be denied or abridged by the United States or by any State on account of sex."*

1919 — Treaty of Versailles Creates Peace

World War I officially ends with the signing of the Treaty of Versailles on June 28, 1919. Negotiated by the Allies with little input from Germany, the treaty is signed in the Hall of Mirrors in the Palace of Versailles in Paris. In retrospect, many believe that the terms of the Versailles Treaty were so tough on the Germans (the imposition of a "War Guilt" clause and heavy debt repayments) that it may have caused the rise of Nazis in Germany and the start of World War II.

This Page:
Above: Snapshot, 1910s.
Below: Snapshot, labeled on the back "Laura & Minnie on rock at the lake, 1915."

Opposite Page:
Studio portrait, young lady in special occasion day dress, 1910s.

1919 — American Anarchist Emma Goldman Gets the Boot

After immigrating to the United States from Lithuania and spending her formative years working in East Coast clothing factories, Emma Goldman becomes a vocal supporter of socialism and anarchy. In 1906, she founds *Mother Earth*, the anarchist periodical she would edit until its suppression in 1917. A fiery orator and prolific writer, Goldman advocates for sexual freedom and birth control, equality and independence for women, radical education, union organization and workers' rights. Post World War I, when unemployment spikes and labor protests escalate, public opinion turns against immigrants and their "foreign" ideas. Goldman and more than 200 other foreign-born radicals are deported to the Soviet Union in 1919.

1919 — Edith Bolling Galt Wilson Takes Charge

President Woodrow Wilson, exhausted from a nationwide tour to promote the League of Nations, an international diplomatic group developed after World War I, suffers a stoke on October 2, 1919. Wilson's wife, Edith Bolling Galt, takes unofficial (and covert) control of the presidency. She hides the true extent of Wilson's incapacitation from the press and his opponents, and insists the she must be the one to screen all the president's paperwork. Mrs. Wilson makes daily decisions about who can meet with her husband and what issues will receive his attention. While there is some suggestion that Edith even signs the president's name to official documents during his recovery, she insists that she is only acting as his steward. (It is never determined how much power she actually wielded.)

From the International Encyclopedia of the First World War:

American losses in World War I were modest compared to those of other belligerents, with 116,516 deaths and approximately 320,000 sick and wounded of the 4.7 million men who served. The U.S. lost more military personnel to disease (63,114) than to combat (53,402), largely due to the influenza epidemic of 1918.

Fashion Footnotes from Photos of the 1910s

The 1910s — "The Era of the Suffragette"

As World War I redefines gender roles in the United States, the notion of women's equality continues to percolate during the 1910s. In response to the changing times, females need a change of clothes. They adopt more streamlined garb, favoring outfits that are better suited to activities ouside the home. For the first time, women also begin designing ladies' clothing. They revolutionize the fashion industry by promoting comfort and casual styles that are perfect for walking, working, and traveling by automobile.

Fashion trends from the decade include:

- Dominant Fashion Idea #1: Freedom from the corset creates a more practical silhouette for modern living.
- Dominant Fashion Idea #2: Hemlines are several inches higher; ankles and insteps are now visible. Skirts are looser and are made of lighter fabrics with gathered folds.
- Hats become smaller, some embellishments persist.
- A slightly higher waistline starts to appear in dresses; hips are smoother and less pronounced.
- The freaky "Hobble Skirt" debuts. It is a streamlined garment with an hem opening so small that it prevents women from walking freely. While the Hobble Skirt uses less fabric, which is good for the war effort, it is an impractical, short-lived trend.
- Some women start to embrace makeup, particularly dark eye shadow.
- The first bobbed hairstyles appear, but they are very daring. Most women cut their hair in the front only and keep it long in back and tied with a ribbon.
- Ladies' Style Icon: Gloria Swanson, silent movie actress
- The new sport of "motoring" in automobiles introduces fashions such as caps with veils, goggles, long coats and scarves to protect ladies from dust and mud.
- By making white garments their visual identifiers, suffragettes adopt a democratic uniform that can be worn by women of any race or social status. White also stands out well in black-and-white newspaper photos and helps draw the attention of the reading public.

This Spread:
Above: Snapshot, lady in a suit, 1910s.
Below: Snapshot, gal by the mailbox, 1910s.
(White dresses also help suffragettes deflect criticism from those who think their behavior is too "masculine" or radical.)
Opposite: Studio portrait, dated 1914.

1920s: Flappers, Speakeasies, Bathtub Gin and Jazz

"She refused to be bored chiefly because she wasn't boring."
— *Zelda Fitzgerald (1900-1948), American flapper, writer, artist, dancer and trendsetter*

After weathering the devastating one-two punch of an overseas war and a flu epidemic, Americans are weary and cynical at the start of the 1920s. A constitutional ban on alcoholic beverages adds to the grim vibe. In response, the nation's focus shifts from political freedom to concern with social and intellectual freedom. People also decide to narcotize their pain by circumventing the law and drinking a whole lot of bootleg liquor.

In 1920, the suffrage movement finally prevails and American women win the right to vote, as specified in the 19th Amendment to the Constitution. The new law's effect is invigorating. It ushers in a decade of free-thinking, free-spirited behavior on the part of young females — many of whom shorten their skirts, bob their hair and smoke cigarettes in public.

Adding fuel to the cultural bonfire, American consumerism is on the rise, influenced by magazines, newspapers, the new medium of radio and Hollywood movies. The practice of buying on credit allows for the increased sales of household goods, clothing and newfangled conveniences like the automobile.

Post-war prosperity inspires everybody to spend money, drink, dance and travel. This social revolution needs a soundtrack all its own; one is joyfully supplied by up-and-coming jazz and blues musicians, Broadway composers, dance bands and orchestras.

Many women can now afford to own vacuum cleaners and carpet sweepers, electric sewing machines and electric irons. Tired of heading to the outdoor pump for a bucket of water? No problem! Indoor plumbing springs up in urban areas first, bringing running water right into the home, along with private toilets, bathtubs and showers. Advances in technology change home meal preparation practices as well. Commercial canned goods, packaged breads and refrigeration eliminate daily trips to the grocer and butcher.

No longer tethered to the kitchen sink, American women explore new leisure pursuits. They swim, ride bicycles, play tennis, hit the ski slopes and hike. Knickers, riding breeches and beach pajamas make ladies' pants seem a bit less scandalous. Life is good. Escapism is fun. This is the American Dream.

This Page:
Above: Studio portrait, 1922.
Below: Snapshot, early 1920s.

Previous Spread:
Left: Snapshot, labeled "May with sedan."
Right: Professional portrait of young lady inscribed "Love From Gladys," 1920s.

1920 — The Allied Powers Try Diplomacy

In response to public demand that something must be done to prevent the kind of widespread suffering and destruction that World War I had created, the League of Nations is founded on January 10, 1920. It is the first international organization dedicated to maintaining world peace through disarmament, negotiation and arbitration. The League of Nations is enacted by the victorious Allied Powers after the Paris Peace Conference.

1920 — Welcome to Prohibition: You're Cut Off!

On January 17, 1920, The National Prohibition Act of 1919, also known as the Volstead Act, becomes the law of the land. Its effects are far-reaching. The act officially makes the sale, transportation, importation and production of liquor illegal in the United States. During the Prohibition Era, this reform reduces the amount of liquor consumed, but also helps create widespread organized criminal activity. Speakeasies abound as Americans find clever new ways to continue drinking alcohol.

1920 — The League of Women Voters Is Founded

At the final meeting of the National American Woman Suffrage Association on March 24, 1919, with the federal suffrage amendment virtually guaranteed, Carrie Chapman Catt proposes a new organization for women voters. The League of Women Voters begins the following year as a "mighty political experiment" that is designed to help 20 million women carry out their new responsibilities as voters and inspire them to use their new power to participate in shaping public policy.

1920 — American Women Win the Long Overdue Right to Vote

More than 70 years after the women's suffrage movement was born in Seneca Falls, New York, Congress finally wakes up and ratifies the 19th Amendment to the Constitution. On August 18, 1920, the work of early feminists Elizabeth Cady Stanton and her friend Lucretia Mott comes to fruition when American women officially earn the right to vote. This landmark victory empowers women and fosters new waves of activism focused on issues such as reproductive rights, sexuality, family, the workplace, child labor, immigration, and gender equality.

1920 — Lois Weber: Big-Time Hollywood Movie Director

Famous Players-Lasky Productions, which ultimately becomes Paramount Pictures, signs female director Lois Weber to a sweetheart of a multi-picture deal. Under its terms, Weber will earn $50,000 and one-third of the profits per film, making her one of the highest paid directors of the day. (Weber also believes that cinema can be used to illuminate complex social issues.)

1920 — Mahjong!

Adventurous tourists and savvy entrepreneurs bring the ancient Chinese game of mahjong to the United States, where it quickly becomes a popular fad. Abercrombie & Fitch takes the lead as the first American company to sell mahjong sets. Played with a set of domino-like tiles, mahjong is a four-person game of skill that involves partnership and strategy. Chinese Americans embrace mahjong as a cultural unifier in a country that still views them as immigrants. Jewish women in New York City play the game while they socialize. Mahjong also has appeal for anyone who wants to learn more about exotic cultures in a globalizing world.

1921 — Coco Chanel Gambles on No. 5 — and Wins Big

After revitalizing women's fashion with sporty, relaxed, corset-free clothing, French couturier Coco Chanel decides to create a perfume for her best clients. Having spent her youth in a convent orphanage, Chanel was taught to be soap-scrubbed and fastidiously clean. (As a result, she is also very vocal about having to work with customers who have body odor.) Chanel hires an acclaimed perfumer named Ernest Beaux, from whom she requests a custom-made fragrance that is both floral and fresh. Several months later, he presents Chanel with 10 different samples he has created for her review. Coco chooses the fifth one — a combination of jasmine, rose, sandalwood and vanilla —and markets Chanel No. 5 as her signature perfume.

Top:
Snapshot, unescorted woman standing on a city street, early 1920s.

Bottom:
Snapshot, woman in a dress with sailor collar, reading a letter, early 1920s.

Above:
Snapshot, no-nonsense woman stopped on an unpaved dirt road, early 1920s.

Below:
Snapshot, three gals in non-farm attire, posing with chickens, early 1920s.

1921 — Edith Wharton: Scandal, Lust and the Upper Crust

Expatriate writer Edith Wharton becomes the first woman to win the Pulitzer Prize for literature in 1921 for her novel, "The Age of Innocence." The book explores the social customs of New York City during the Gilded Age and examines issues of duty, honor, family traditions and (gasp!) forbidden love. Wharton's novel establishes her credentials as a writer and chronicles the passing of an era.

1921 — Eleanor Roosevelt Helps FDR Fight Polio

After bearing six children and discovering that her husband, Franklin Delano Roosevelt, is having an affair with her social secretary, Eleanor Roosevelt is disillusioned with her marriage. However, when Franklin, a practicing New York attorney, suffers a near-fatal bout with polio in 1921, Eleanor steps up to nurse him and save his political career. She gives speeches and makes public appearances on his behalf. Eleanor also works with the Women's Trade Union League (WTUL) in support of a 48-hour work week, minimum wage and the abolition of child labor. Eleanor's efforts help Franklin win the election as Governor of New York in 1928.

1921 — The Emergency Quota Act Is Signed

In response to a growing anti-immigration movement, Americans begin to push the federal government to restrict the number of foreigners who can enter the country. On May 19, 1921, the same day on which the Emergency

Quota Act is passed by the U.S. Congress, President Warren G. Harding signs it into law. The act establishes a temporary system to limit immigration and uses statistics from the 1910 census to severely curb immigration from countries other than those in Northern Europe.

1921 — Bessie Coleman Proves That the Sky's the Limit

When no flight schools in the United States would enroll her as an African-American woman, Bessie Coleman learns to speak French and moves to France. She earns her international pilot's license on June 15, 1921 and gains additional flying experience so she can perform in air shows. Coleman specializes in stunt flying and parachuting, and earns a living barnstorming and performing aerial tricks. As the first African-American woman to hold a pilot's license, Coleman becomes a pioneer in the field of aviation.

1921 — Miss America Pageant Entertains Atlantic City Tourists

In an effort to keep tourists in Atlantic City, New Jersey, after the 1920 Labor Day weekend, promoters stage a "Fall Frolic." The city-wide festival features a rolling chair parade down the famed Boardwalk. In 1921, the organizers decide to add a beauty contest to their high-spirited parade on wheels. This second incarnation attracts an even bigger crowd on September 7 and 8, and is known thereafter as the first-ever Miss America Pageant. The winner, Margaret Gorman, is proclaimed the "Most Beautiful Bathing Girl in America," and goes home with the coveted "Golden Mermaid" trophy.

1921 — Meet Betty: A Mythical Female Authority Figure

The fictional character Betty Crocker is created in October 1921 by the Washburn-Crosby Company after a contest in the *Saturday Evening Post*. Little more than a cartoon, Betty acts as the spokeswoman who can publicly answer consumer questions and make product recommendations. She eventually becomes the face of the General Mills Corporation and is a staple in advertising the brand. Betty Crocker's red spoon logo and her "Betty Seal of Approval" evolve into symbols of culinary excellence.

1922 — Abbreviated News for On-the-Go Readers

A pocket-sized monthly magazine, *Reader's Digest* captures the reading public's attention by offering condensed versions of articles taken from other periodicals. Founded on a shoestring budget in February 1922 by DeWitt Wallace and his wife, Lila Bell Acheson, *Reader's Digest* appeals to consumers and eventually becomes the highest circulating general interest magazine in the United States. *Reader's Digest* is conservative in editorial tone and presents itself as the guardian of American morality and values.

Above:
Snapshot, three ladies in fashionable hats and special occasion dresses, 1920s.

Below:
Snapshot, young woman carrying two thermoses, 1920s.

Above:
Snapshot, young woman in winter coat posing with a deer, 1920s.

Below:
Snapshot, mature woman in exotic ensemble, with pearls and fan, 1920s.

1922 — Abraham Lincoln Immortalized in Washington, D.C.

On Memorial Day, May 30, 1922, the Lincoln Memorial is dedicated — some 57 years after President Abraham Lincoln's assassination. The centerpiece of the monument is a 19-foot statue of Lincoln by Daniel Chester French, the leading American sculptor of the day. Some 50,000 people attend the ceremonies, including hundreds of Civil War veterans and Robert Todd Lincoln, the president's only surviving son. The inscription on the building reads: "In this temple, as in the hearts of the people for whom he saved the Union, the memory of Abraham Lincoln is enshrined forever."

1922 — Anna May Wong: An Actress on the Rise

Chinese-American actress Anna May Wong, age 17, stars in "The Toll of the Sea," the first wide-release Technicolor silent movie, which premieres on November 26, 1922. Wong plays Lotus Flower, a girl who rescues an American man from the sea, falls in love and marries him, even though their cross-cultural relationship is doomed. Ambitious and stylish in real life, Wong struggles to transcend these stereotypical roles, which are all that Hollywood offers her. Wong heads to Europe and hangs out in the Weimar Republic, where she becomes fluent in German, Italian and French. She continuously travels between the United States and Europe for stage and film work. By 1932, Wong is an international movie star, working with Marlene Dietrich in the hugely successful "Shanghai Express."

1922 — "Tutmania" Fires Up Women's Fashion

British archaeologist Howard Carter and his financial backer George Herbert, the Earl of Carnarvon, open King Tutankhamen's Tomb on November 26, 1922. Their discovery in the Valley of the Kings launches an advertising frenzy that makes Egyptian-themed music, dance, art and fashion all the rage. The lotus motif begins to appear in American dress designs, and chic women adopt beaded headpieces, tunic-style ensembles and snake bracelets. Department stores introduce new, dark eye shadow and lipstick shades inspired by ancient Egyptian decorative arts.

1923 — Alice Paul Proposes an Equal Rights Amendment

After having been a pivotal force in the passage and ratification in 1920 of the 19th Amendment, American suffragist Alice Paul proves again that she won't take 'no' for an answer. In conjunction with the 75th anniversary of the Seneca Falls Convention, Paul proposes an Equal Rights Amendment. She believes that the ERA will remedy inequalities not addressed in the 19th Amendment. Paul's initial version of the ERA proclaims that, "Men and women shall have equal rights throughout the United States and every place subject to its jurisdiction."

1923 — The Rosewood Massacre

In January 1923, a racially-motivated riot decimates the town of Rosewood in rural Levy County, Florida. The trouble begins after a white woman claims that a black man assaulted her in her home. A lynch mob, drawing vigilantes from neighboring communities, descends on the primarily African-American town. As the conflict escalates, homes, businesses and churches are burned to the ground. Many residents run for their lives and seek refuge in the nearby swampland. Horrific violence ensues. The official death toll is six, but eyewitnesses claim that it's closer to 150. Survivors are evacuated by train and car and none return to Rosewood. The ruined town is abandoned by its former residents, black and white alike.

1923 — Early Experiments with Movies and Sound

In the Rivoli Theatre in New York City, American inventor Lee De Forest presents the first sound-on-film motion picture on April 15, 1923. With De Forest's rudimentary system, the soundtrack is photographically recorded onto the side of the strip of motion picture film to create a composite print. If sound and picture are correctly synced during the recording process, it could be recreated in playback.

1923 — U.S. Supreme Court Strikes Down Minimum Wage Laws

In the case of *Adkins v. Children's Hospital*, the Supreme Court rules that a minimum wage law for women was unconstitutional because it abridged a citizen's right to freely contract labor. Five years earlier, the District of Columbia had passed a law setting the minimum wage for women and children to protect them from "conditions detrimental to their health and morals, resulting from wages which are inadequate to maintain decent standards of living." The Children's Hospital, which employed many women at substandard wages, sues and wins on appeal.

1923 — Roll Your Stockings Down, Doll: It's the Charleston!

Rather than embracing the traditional dance steps that their parents favored — including the waltz, the two-step or the polka — in the 1920s, young women and men dance the Charleston. The dance becomes all the rage after it's featured in the 1923 Broadway musical "Runnin' Wild." Along with drinking, smoking and necking in parked automobiles, it symbolizes the uninhibited moral code of the new generation.

1924 — Waitress Works Late, Winds Up in Court

When her husband left to fight in World War I, Anna Smith needed to earn a living as a waitress. Her employer, Joseph Radice & Co. in Buffalo, New

This Page:
Top: Studio portrait printed on postcard, inscribed "Sister Reid, April 1922."

Bottom: Postcard mailing side, stamped April 23, 1922. Handwritten message reads:
"Oh Dear, How I am
Thinking of you
Please do not let any one see this
ugly potor [*sic*]:
I had it made in the night
Your Sister RM"

(According to the U.S. Postal Service, more than 206 million postcards were sent via first-class mail in 1926. Real Photo Postcards (RPPCs) needed a one-cent postage stamp.)

York, allowed her to wait tables past 10 p.m. if she wanted to make extra money. She did. An inspector begs to differ and fines Radice for violating a state law that forbids women from working as waitresses between 10 p.m. and 6 a.m. (A statute that was enacted to protect women's health and well-being.) Radice pleads not guilty and her case eventually goes to the U.S. Supreme Court. In *Radice v. New York,* the court upholds the law, sides with the state, and decides for Anna Smith what is in her best interest in terms of the hours she is able to work to earn a living.

1924 — Native Americans Officially Recognized as U.S. Citizens

With the passage of the Indian Citizenship Act on June 2, 1924, the U.S. government declares that all Native Americans born within the territorial limits of the country are citizens. The act is signed into law by President Calvin Coolidge in order to recognize the thousands of Indians who served in the armed forces in World War I. Many other indigenous people had already become citizens by giving up tribal affiliations or assimilating into mainstream American life. Even after the passage of the act, the privileges of citizenship — including the right to vote — remain largely governed by state law and are frequently denied to Native Americans.

1924 — Macy's Struts Its Stuff

The first Macy's Thanksgiving Day Parade is held on November 27, 1924 in New York City. The procession stretches for two blocks and features nursery rhyme characters, a nod to the Macy's Christmas window displays, which are spiffed up for the season. Led by police escort, the parade kicks off at 145th Street and Convent Avenue in Harlem and travels all the way to Herald Square in Midtown. Animals on loan from the Central Park Zoo — bears, elephants, camels and monkeys — add to the festivities. Macy's employees march as well, and are dressed as clowns, gypsies, cowboys and knights in shining armor. Santa and his reindeer appear at the parade's end, with greetings for everyone, both the naughty and the nice.

1925 — Anita Loos Explains Why Gentlemen Prefer Blondes

On a cross-country train trip, brunette Hollywood screenwriter Anita Loos notices that a blonde female passenger receives considerably more attention from the male passengers than she does. The experience inspires her to write the comic novella "Gentlemen Prefer Blondes: The Intimate Diary of a Professional Lady," which becomes famous for depicting the Prohibition Era. Decades later, the madcap adventures of Loos' jewelry-loving protagonist, Lorelei Lee, will come to life on the Broadway stage (with Carol Channing in 1949) and in a big-budget Hollywood movie (with Marilyn Monroe in 1953).

This Page:
Top: Snapshot, Native American woman posing in traditional dress, 1920s.

Bottom: Snapshot, young woman in casual outfit, leaning on car fender, 1920s.

Opposite Page:
Studio portrait, young woman in elegant dress and patterned stockings, 1920s

Above:
Snapshot, women in fancy bonnets holding floral bouquets, early 1920s.

Below:
Snapshot, inscribed on back as "Grandma Nettie, 1920s."

1925 — Josephine Baker: The Toast of Paris

African-American singer/dancer Josephine Baker leaves the segregated United States behind and takes her act overseas to France. Leveraging the popularity of American jazz, the free-spirited Baker introduces her *"danse sauvage"* to Parisian audiences who love not only her talent, but her propensity for wearing little more than a skirt made of feathers. Baker goes one step further at the Folies-Bergere, where she performs in a G-string covered in bananas. She becomes the most highly-paid performer in Europe.

1925 — There's Something for Everyone at Sears!

After succeeding in the catalog shopping business since 1893, Sears, Roebuck & Co. shifts gears and opens its first retail store in Chicago in 1925. The emporium is housed in the company's sprawling Merchandise Building on the city's West Side. Designed to serve both men and women, Sears offers hardware, furniture and building materials as well as practical, durable clothing. An optical shop and a soda fountain add to its appeal for working-class families.

1925 — The Scopes "Monkey Trial" Begins

Substitute teacher John T. Scopes, who is accused of teaching Charles Darwin's theory of evolution in a Dayton, Tennessee high school, goes on trial on July 10, 1925. He is accused of violating Tennessee's Butler Act, which makes is illegal to teach human evolution in any state-funded school. The famed attorney Clarence Darrow, working with the ACLU, defends

Scopes. The trial essentially becomes a public debate on whether science (human knowledge) should take priority over the word of God (the Bible) in American school curriculum. The topic manages to draw the ire of both urban sophisticates and rural Christians. When the trial ends on July 21, and Scopes is fined just $100, monkeys everywhere breathe a sigh of relief.

Above:
Snapshot, lineup of seven young ladies in nearly identical hats, early 1920s.

1925 — F. Scott Fitzgerald Publishes "The Great Gatsby"

Using dialogue inspired by the witticisms of his charasmatic wife, Zelda, F. Scott Fitzgerald creates the unattainable golden-girl character of Daisy Buchanan in his novel "The Great Gatsby." Set in the fictional Long Island towns of East and West Egg in the summer of 1922, the book weaves a cautionary tale of ambition, honor and lost love. Perhaps more than any other American novel, Fitzgerald's "Gatsby" captures the wild abandon — and recklessness — associated with Jazz Age prosperity and wealth.

Below:
Snapshot, Red Crown Gasoline, 1920s.

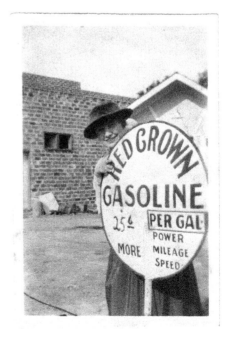

1925 — Country Music Finds a New Showcase

The Grand Ole Opry transmits its first radio broadcast on November 28, 1925 from its fifth-floor studio in the National Life & Accident Insurance Company building in Nashville, Tennessee. The company had originally built a radio station as a public service in the hopes that the new medium could advertise its insurance policies. History is made when the announcer on radio station WSM (which stands for "We Shield Millions") introduces "The WSM Barn Dance" and 77-year-old fiddle player Uncle Jimmy Thompson kicks off the inaugural show.

Above:
Casual portrait printed on postcard, 1920s.

Below:
Snapshot, woman at the roadside, inscribed "San Antonio" on back, 1920s.

1926 — The First Scholastic Aptitude Test (SAT)

Some 8,000 prospective college freshmen take the very first SAT admissions test on June 23, 1926. They have just 97 minutes to complete 315 multiple-choice questions in nine categories including Definitions, Arithmetic, Logical Inference and Paragraph Reading. Each candidate received a test-prep booklet one week before the exam. Sixty percent of the test-takers are male and of these candidates, 26 percent apply to Yale University. Of the female test-takers, 27 percent use their SAT scores to apply to Smith College.

1926 — Dorothy Parker: A Professional Smart-Ass

Algonquin Round Table wit Dorothy Parker publishes her first collection of poetry, "Enough Rope" in 1926. Though the *New York Times* dismisses it as "flapper verse," it becomes a bestseller. In her role as a contributing editor with *The New Yorker*, Parker also achieves popularity with book reviews published under the byline "Constant Reader." The hard-drinking Parker is no fan of cutesy sentiment and whimsy. In her assessment of A.A. Milne's "The House at Pooh Corner," she writes: "Tonstant Weader fwowed up."

1926 — Get Your Kicks on Route 66

One of the original U.S. highways, Route 66 is established in the summer of 1926, though official road signs do not appear until 1927. Route 66 is the primary route for people traveling west and its diagonal course is instrumental to the growth of the U.S. trucking industry. The need for fuel, food and lodging along the way gives rise to many small businesses and makes entire towns prosper. Route 66 begins in Chicago, Illinois, and winds though Missouri, Kansas, Oklahoma, Texas, New Mexico and Arizona. It ends near Los Angeles, California, making it 2,448 miles from start to finish.

1926 — Gertrude Ederle: Queen of the Waves!

American Olympic champion Gertrude Ederle breaks a new record on August 6, 1926, when she becomes the first woman to swim across the English Channel. The feat takes 14 hours and 34 minutes. Upon her return home, Ederle is greeted with a ticker-tape parade in Manhattan that draws an estimated 2 million spectators.

1926 — The Real Ladies Behind the Cell Block Tango

Former *Chicago Tribune* reporter Maurine Dallas Watkins writes a stage play based on two sensational murder trials she covers while on assignment in the Windy City. Blending the true stories of Belva Gaertner, a divorced cabaret singer, and Beulah Annan, a housewife with a boyfriend on the side, Watkins creates "The Brave Little Woman." After some tweaking, her play

opens in 1926 under the name "Chicago." The story of two trigger-happy women who (allegedly) murder the men in their lives captures the essence of the jazz-and-booze-fueled Roaring Twenties. Watkins' play also illustrates how the fictional Velma Kelly and Roxie Hart were able to manipulate the media, achieve redemption in the court of public opinion, and walk free.

1926 — NBC Starts Its Radio Broadcasts

The Radio Corporation of America (RCA) puts up half the dough and joins with partners General Electric and Westinghouse to create the NBC Radio Network. On November 15, 1926, NBC begins broadcasting with a live gala from the Waldorf-Astoria in New York. Within a year, it is operating the Red Network (for commercially sponsored music and entertainment) and the Blue Network (non-sponsored news and cultural programs).

1927 — The Great Mississippi Flood Displaces Thousands

More than 640,000 people from Illinois to Louisiana are affected by massive flooding in the areas surrounding the Mississippi River. The waters cover 16 million acres of land and it's estimated that in Vicksburg, Mississippi, the river swells to 80 miles wide. The majority of people displaced are African-Americans, who have to live in relief camps for long periods of time. As a result, many families leave the agricultural South altogether, joining the Great Migration to industrial cities in the Northern and Midwestern states.

Clothing for Active, Sporty Gals!
Top: Snapshot, tennis attire, early 1920s
Bottom: Snapshot, "middy" blouse and knickers, late 1920s or early 1930s.

This Page:
Women's clothing (and their morals) become more casual and free-spirited during the 1920s. Americans have time for leisure activities and money to burn!
Above: Snapshot, sports uniforms.
Right: Snapshot, swimming hole attire.
Below: Snapshot, riding jodhpurs.

1927 — Lucky Lindy Defies the Odds in the Spirit of St. Louis

Charles Lindbergh leaves Roosevelt Field in New York on the first solo non-stop, trans-Atlantic flight on May 20, 1927. His custom-built, single-engine monoplane carries 451 gallons of gas, as well as four sandwiches and two canteens of water for the pilot. After struggling to stay awake and experiencing hallucinations while flying over the Atlantic Ocean, Lindbergh reaches Paris in a little over 33.5 hours.

1927 — Al Jolson Takes a Bow in "The Jazz Singer"

The first full-length feature film to blend a soundtrack, dialogue and some lip-synching, "The Jazz Singer" effectively ends the silent movie era. Stage actor Al Jolson plays conflicted protagonist, singer Jakie Rabinowitz, who reconciles with his cantor father on his death bed, then appears in blackface to end the movie with a performance of "My Mammy." At the time of the film's release, fewer than 100 theaters in the world were equipped for sound.

1928 — Amelia Earhart Promotes Women in Aviation

After she joins pilots Wilmer Stultz and Louis Gordon as a passenger on the Fokker Friendship, Amelia Earhart earns the designation of being the first woman to fly across the Atlantic Ocean. The ensuing celebrity she receives annoys her since she was only allowed to keep the logbook on the flight. While she accepts the invitation to gain publicity for women in the field of aviation, her passive role in the flight makes her disgusted enough to compare her presence to being like "baggage" or "a sack of potatoes."

Opposite Page:
Formal studio portrait, 1920s.
(Of course, a gal could still dress up!)

This Page:
Above: Snapshot, all-girl pyramid, 1920s.
Below: Portrait, lady with flowers, 1920s.

Opposite Page:
Top: Sassy lady with wedding cake, 1920s.
Bottom: California flapper, 1920s.

1928 — The Greatest Thing Since Sliced Bread!

In Chillicothe, Missouri, a bakery begins to use Otto Frederick Rohwedder's automatic bread slicing machine. This small development in the realm of food preparation is a timesaver for housewives and a boon to anyone else who wants a sandwich. In order to keep the slices from getting tossed about and crumpled inside the bag during shipping, a pin is inserted in the loaf to keep it together. Americans wholeheartedly embrace sliced bread not only because it's convenient, but because the uniform slices fit neatly into their newfangled electric pop-up toasters.

1928 — Margaret Mead Studies a Neurosis-Free Zone for Girls

Anthropologist Margaret Mead, who is interested in discovering whether adolescence is a stressful experience for young girls in remote cultures, journeys to Samoa in 1925. She ponders the topics of nature vs. nurture, family relationships, gender roles and cultural attitudes. Mead concludes that the transition from girlhood to maturity in Samoa does not involve the same levels of angst and psychological trauma that one finds in the United States. The end result of Mead's research is the publication in 1928 of her most famous book, "Coming of Age in Samoa."

1928 — The Radium Girls Shine Their Own Light

During the 1920s, the U.S. Radium Corporation in New Jersey employs working-class women as watch-dial painters. The wages are high — and so are the stakes in regard to one's health. The "Radium Girls" are encouraged to "lip-point" their tiny paintbrushes in their mouths before dipping them in luminescent, radium-based paint. By doing so, they swallow minute quantities of radium every single day. By 1927, more than 50 women have died from the horrific effects of radium poisoning. Five more, led by 25-year-old Grace Fryer, file a lawsuit. (Fryer attends the legal proceedings, but cannot walk unassisted and has lost all her teeth.) U.S. Radium settles out of court and The Radium Girls help establish new safety standards for all American industrial workers.

1928 — My Name Ain't "Baby" — It's Minnie!

Walt Disney's famous Mickey and Minnie Mouse cartoon characters appear for the first time in 1928 in the animated short film "Steamboat Willie." Minnie is a kind, sweet and fashionable sort of female. Created by Walt Disney and Ub Iwerks to be the object of Mickey's affection, Minnie wears a short, flapper-style dress that often reveals her patched knickers. She is also known to favor oversized high-heeled shoes — perfect for clomping around and dancing! By 1929, Minnie is shown wearing black stockings, a fashion trend that is popular with flappers.

This Spread:
Above: Photo booth image, woman in cloche hat and fur collar.
Opposite Page: Studio portrait of woman with bobbed hair and drop-waist dress.
Below: Snapshot, ladies in cloche hats, posing in front of elaborate architecture.
All images from mid- to late 1920s.

1929 — St. Valentine's Day Massacre

Illegal activity in Chicago, Illinois, has flourished under Prohibition, due in part to bootlegger Alphonse Capone's criminal genius. By bribing police and politicians and marshaling an army of delivery truck drivers, salespeople and bodyguards, Capone has created a well-oiled liquor distribution machine. And he doesn't like competition. On February 14, 1929, a delivery of bootleg whiskey is expected at rival gangster Bugs Moran's headquarters at the SMC Cartage Garage on Clark Street in Chicago. Four men, two dressed as police officers, enter the garage and execute seven members of Moran's gang. The killers, who are believed to be working for Capone, line their victims up against a brick wall and gun them down. It is estimated that 70 rounds of ammunition are fired. Capone himself has an ironclad alibi: He is in Florida at the time of the massacre. The crime remains unsolved.

1929 — Wall Street Crashes, Billions of Dollars Are Lost

Even though the stock market is rapidly expanding during the 1920s, rising unemployment, low wages, a struggling agricultural sector and the proliferation of debt set the stage for big economic trouble. Stock prices begin to decline in September and panic ensues. The postwar prosperity of the Roaring Twenties comes to a screeching halt on October 29, 1929 — a date that becomes known as Black Tuesday. The Stock Market Crash starts The Great Depression, which devastates the United States and impacts all Western industrialized nations for the next decade.

1929 — Women Pilots Organize The Ninety-Nines, Inc.

On November 2, 1929, a group of women pilots meet in a hangar at the Curtiss Field on Long Island, New York, to create an organization that will be open only to female pilots. They settle on "The Ninety-Nines, Inc." as their official name because that represents their charter membership. They assemble for mutual support and to promote the advancement of women as professional aviators. Together, they find strength in numbers.

Fashion Footnotes from Photos of the 1920s

The 1920s — "The Roaring Twenties"

One of the more widely recognized decades in terms of fashion, the 1920s represents the birth of the modern woman. The long-awaited ratification of the 19th Amendment not only gives ladies the right to vote and a voice regarding the way the country should be run, it sets the tone for their words, actions and deeds in the years ahead. Women can vote, work and party!

Fashion trends from the decade include:

- Dominant Fashion Idea #1: The cloche hat is the bomb! Small, sleek and bell-shaped, it is flattering for women of all ages. The stylish hat derives its name from the French word *cloche*, which means "bell."
- Dominant Fashion Idea #2: By the end of the decade, hemlines rise to the knee and women's legs are visible for the first time. The hosiery business booms and novelty stockings become extremely popular. Stockings are made of cotton, silk or wool.
- Dominant Fashion Idea #3: The shift dress dominates. It provides a streamlined silhouette that is not about looking feminine and curvy. Arms are often bare. Accents include feather boas and long necklaces.
- Dominant Fashion Idea #4: In keeping with the bold and rebellious attitudes of the day, bobbed hair becomes the norm. Decorative headbands and fancy scarves add interest to the new short hairdos.
- Dark eye makeup and bee-stung lips are the trends in cosmetics.
- Dominant Aesthetic of the Day: Art Deco is is all the rage in visual arts, fashion and architecture. It is modern, geometric and bold.
- In response to aggressive marketing on the part of tobacco companies, the go-to fashion accessory for liberated women is the cigarette.
- Ladies' Style Icons: Silent movie actresses Clara Bow, Louise Brooks, Colleen Moore, Mary Pickford and Gloria Swanson.
- Coco Chanel introduces the "Little Black Dress," a minimalist garment that pairs easily with daytime, cocktail hour or evening accessories.

This Spread:
Above: Snapshot, women with bobbed hair seated on snowy porch, 1920s; Below: Snapshot, woman in cloche hat and fur collar shows a lot of leg, 1920s; Opposite Page: Studio portrait, young lady in elaborate formal dress, pearls and stylish headband, early 1920s.

1930s: The Great Depression, Dust Storms and The New Deal

"It ain't no sin if you crack a few laws now and then, just so long as you don't break any."

— *Mae West (1893-1980), American actress, singer, comedian, playwright and sex symbol*

Talk about a buzzkill. Just when life was getting interesting, with all the dancing, drinking and rising hemlines, the stock market crash in October 1929 pulls the plug on everything. Anxious Americans tighten their belts at the first sign of trouble. The wealthy quickly take their assets out of the economy. Average consumers, in turn, spend less and save whatever they can. Bankruptcies and foreclosures escalate, as does the nation's unemployment rate. Family farms and businesses are lost and thousands of banks fail.

The Great Depression defines the 1930s and impacts the entire industrialized Western world. Across the United States, impoverished Americans establish shantytowns called "Hoovervilles," named in honor of President Herbert Hoover. Gangs of roving criminals achieve celebrity status for bank robbing, assorted stickups and evading law enforcement, with their heists sensationalized in media coverage.

American women cut corners wherever possible. They patch and sew clothing, grow their own produce and take any menial job that will put food on the table. Macaroni, beans and one-pot stews abound. A common slogan of the era urges Americans to "Use it up, wear it out, make it do, or do without."

Comic books, magazines and a steady stream of Hollywood movies provide low-cost entertainment for people seeking respite from the everyday grind. Board games such as "Monopoly" and "Scrabble" make their debuts. The radio becomes the central piece of furniture in the home, with families gathering to enjoy live programs like "The Shadow" or "The Lone Ranger." There might not be an evening gown in her closet, but an American woman can catch a big band remote broadcast on the radio and pretend she's at a swanky New York hotel with the beautiful people.

The decade is further enriched by the birth of the Hostess Twinkie (1930), Skippy Peanut Butter (1932), Ritz Crackers and Hawaiian Punch (1934) and Spam (1937). Luckily, the "plop, plop, fizz, fizz" of Alka-Seltzer antacid was also introduced in 1931.

1930 — ASWPL Women Work to Eliminate the Crime of Lynching

Texas civil-rights activist Jessie Daniel Ames believes that women can solve the South's racial problems. To that end, she rallies thousands of middle-class and wealthy white women and forms The Association of Southern Women for the Prevention of Lynching. Ames makes the case that lynching is a vicious and indefensible crime, committed in the name of protecting white women from rape, but one actually motivated by racism and hatred.

1930 — Discovery of Pluto, the Ninth Planet

At the Lowell Observatory in Flagstaff, Arizona, the American astronomer Clyde Tombaugh discovers Pluto on February 18, 1930. Tombaugh detects the distant orb with a new technique that combines photographic plates and a blink microscope. The observatory then holds a naming contest. Eleven-year-old Venetia Burney, of Oxford, England, suggests calling the tiny planet "Pluto," after the Roman God of the underworld, a mythical guy who has the power of invisibility. Coincidentally, in 1931, Mickey Mouse's cartoon dog, "Pluto the Pup," is officially introduced to the public.

1930 — Poverty: The Great Motivator

The effects of The Great Depression are so devastating that they create major shifts in economic theory and government policy. The damage also extends beyond American borders. Due to poverty and social unrest around the world, political ideologies such as Fascism, Nazism, and extreme Communism gain popularity.

1930 — The First Stewardess Gets Her Wings

Working around the sexism of the day, registered nurse and licensed pilot Ellen Church lobbies for a position with Boeing Air Transport and becomes a flight attendant. Realizing that she will never be hired as a pilot, the 25-year-old Church settles for hauling luggage, serving refreshments and helping show the public that air travel is safe. Her first flight (Oakland to Chicago) takes 20 hours, makes 13 stops and carries 14 passengers.

1930 — Necessity: The Mother of the CCC

Oh, blessed turn of events! Mrs. Ruth Wakefield, a dietitian, lecturer and accomplished foodie is baking a batch traditional colonial "Chocolate Butter Drop Do" cookies for her guests at the Toll House Inn in Whitman, Massachusetts, when she realizes she is out of baker's chocolate. Wakefield pinch hits by chopping up a block of semi-sweet Nestle's Chocolate for her recipe. Instead of melting, the chunks stay chippy and gooey and a new dessert treat is born. The Nestle Company takes note as well when Mrs.

Above:
Snapshots, 1930s.

Previous Spread:
Right: Souvenir photo, October, 1931.
Left: Snapshot, Art Deco border, 1930s.

Wakefield's cookies become enormously popular and sales of its semi-sweet chocolate go through the roof. The company agrees to print the Toll House Cookie recipe on its packaging and Mrs. Wakefield receives a lifetime supply of Nestle's chocolate as compensation.

1931 — The Drought Years Begin

A severe drought hits the Midwestern and the Southern Plain states. Conditions are particularly brutal in western Kansas, eastern Colorado, northeastern New Mexico and the Oklahoma and Texas panhandles. For decades, farmers had removed the land's natural grass sod in order to plant wheat. As a result, the over-plowed and over-grazed terrain cannot sustain crops. When the prairie winds sweep across the region, tons of black dirt are whirled into the air, creating "black blizzards." The impact of the Great Depression, coupled with the effects of the drought (1931-1939), completely destroys many farming communities.

1931 — Oh, Say Can You See?

After gaining popularity during the 1800s, the "Star-Spangled Banner" is named the national anthem of the United States of America on March 3, 1931. (Other contenders for the honor were "My Country, 'Tis of Thee," and "America the Beautiful.") President Herbert Hoover and an act of Congress

Above:
Silver-gelatin print, woman and boy feeding ducks, Sussex County, 1930s.

Below:
Snapshot, woman on motorcycle, late 1920s or early 1930s.

Above:
Snapshot, laundry day photo, 1930s.

Below:
Snapshot, rock pile ladies, 1930s.

make the designation official, but the feeling lingers among many that the song is too high-pitched for the average citizen to sing. The lyrics of the anthem, written in 1814 by Francis Scott Key, were inspired by the sight of the American flag still flying over Fort McHenry at Baltimore Harbor after a night of heavy British bombardment.

1931 — The Empire State Building: An Art Deco Wonder

In the midst of the Great Depression's misery, the Empire State Building rises as a symbol of American pride and hope. On May 1, 1931, President Hoover presses a button in Washington, D.C. to turn on its lights and officially open the building. At 102 stories and 1,454 feet tall at the top of its lightning rod, it is the world's tallest skyscraper. The $40 million project is completed in just over a year. The construction process had employed as many as 3,400 workers on any given day — a much-coveted gig, given the economic climate of the time. However, one year later, only 25 percent of the Empire State Building's office space is occupied.

1931 — Scarface Learns that the Taxman Cometh for Us All

Alphonse Capone, the publicity-loving gangster known by the nickname "Scarface," is convicted of tax evasion on October 18, 1931. He is sentenced to 11 years in federal prison and fined $50,000 plus court costs. Capone is also held liable for $215,000 plus interest due on back taxes. These legal entanglements effectively put an end to Capone's career as the ruthless and larger-than-life boss of the Chicago crime syndicate.

1931 — Jane Addams Wins the Nobel Peace Prize

In addition to founding the Women's International League for Peace and Freedom in 1919, Jane Addams runs Hull House in Chicago, a settlement house that helps the urban poor. The original mission of Hull House was to offer educational programs for immigrants, but as time passes, Addams sees that they need social and cultural services as well. Hull House becomes an incubator for progressive social programs and provides a nursery school, public kitchen, library, gymnasium and art gallery. Addams writes and lectures extensively; the methods she uses at Hull House are studied and emulated in the field of social work.

1932 — Introducing Senator Caraway

Hattie Wyatt Caraway (D-Ark.) becomes the first woman in the U.S. Senate in January of 1932, when she wins a special election to replace her recently deceased husband, Thaddeus Caraway. Her observation upon entering the Senate chamber for the first time is, "The windows need washing!" Before the general election rolls around later in the year, "Silent Hattie" enlists the help of not-so-silent Louisiana politician Huey P. Long in order to bolster her campaign. They tour Arkansas together and Caraway wins in a landslide.

1932 — A Family Tragedy: The Lindbergh Kidnapping

On March 1, 1932, Charles Augustus Lindbergh Jr., the infant son of aviator Charles Lindbergh and his wife, Anne Morrow Lindbergh, is abducted from his New Jersey home. The boy, who is almost two years old, is put to bed in his crib by his nanny around 7:30 p.m. Several hours later, when she returns to check on him, the child is missing. The family finds a kidnapper's note and pays a $50,000 ransom, but on May 12, the boy's lifeless body is found in the woods not far from the Lindbergh estate. Three years later, Bruno Hauptmann, a German-born carpenter, is convicted of the crime and sentenced to death in the electric chair.

1932 — Amelia Earhart Proves She's a Complete Badass

By piloting her Lockheed Vega monoplane on May 21-22, 1932, from Harbor Grace, Newfoundland to Culmore, Ireland, Amelia Earhart becomes the first woman to complete a solo flight across the Atlantic Ocean. She is also the first aviator to fly nonstop and alone on such a journey since Charles Lindbergh had done so in 1927. Not one to rest on her laurels, Earhart becomes the first woman to fly solo and nonstop across the U.S., from Los Angeles to Newark, New Jersey, in about 19 hours on August 24–25, 1932.

Above:
Snapshot, labeled "October, 1932."

Below:
Studio portrait, graduate with diploma and hair styled in Marcel waves, 1930s.

Above:
Snapshot, woman in the garden, 1930s.

Below:
Snapshot, The Willamette National Forest was established in its current form in 1933 as part of New Deal efforts.

1932 — Trouble and Dust Blanket the Heartland

With no end in sight to the brutal drought conditions, the dust storms in the Great Plains escalate. More than 14 are reported in 1932. The next year, there will be 38. The combination of an increased use of mechanized farm equipment and a lack of understanding of the ecology of the plains exacerbate the problem. During these dust storms, the choking clouds of black dirt reduce visibility to three feet on the plains. Farm families seal their windows and hang wet sheets over their doorways. Those who venture outside wear handkerchiefs, face masks and goggles and rub Vaseline into their nostrils to protect from the dust. Birds, small animals and livestock suffocate in the blowing dirt.

1933 — FDR Is Inaugurated for the First Time

Franklin Delano Roosevelt becomes President of the United States on March 4, 1933. His inaugural address tells Americans that the "only thing we have to fear is fear itself." Armed with charisma and a can-do attitude, FDR begins the process of rallying Congress and the public to begin rebuilding that nation during the Great Depression. In order to communicate his agenda to the electorate, FDR starts giving his evening radio addresses, known as "Fireside Chats," eight days after taking office. At the time of FDR's Inaugural, "Happy Days Are Here Again" is popular on the radio. (Nobody believes the song.)

- In 40 of the 48 states, all the banks are closed.
- The New York Stock Exchange has suspended trading.
- Industrial production has been cut by almost 50 percent.
- Nearly half of all American families face foreclosure.
- Almost 1 in 4 wage earners are out of work, both male and female.
- About 40 million people have no dependable source of income.
- Half of all African-Americans are out of work.
- The 400,000 African-Americans who join in "The Great Migration" to the Northern states find no jobs there, either. What they do encounter is dangerous, unchecked hostility on the part of the unemployed white residents in the North. (Until 1910, more than 90 percent of the African-American population lived in the Southern states.)

1933 — Frances Perkins: The First Female Cabinet Member

A longtime advocate for working women, Frances Perkins is appointed as the Secretary of Labor in Franklin Delano Roosevelt's administration. As a loyal supporter of FDR, Perkins helps bring the labor movement — including minimum-wage laws — into the New Deal efforts. Perkins and Interior Secretary Harold L. Ickes are the only original Roosevelt cabinet members to remain in office for his entire presidency, until 1945.

1933 — Billie Holiday Steps into the Spotlight in New York City

While performing in a Harlem jazz club, 18-year-old Billie Holiday attracts the attention of record producer John Hammond, a lifelong crusader for integration in the music business. Impressed with Holiday's unique vocal stylings, he produces her debut recordings for Columbia Records. Holiday begins her legendary career by cutting two songs with Benny Goodman and his Orchestra: "Your Mother's Son-in-Law" and "Riffin' the Scotch," the latter of which sells 5,000 copies. Holiday's next big break would be an onscreen appearance as a rejected, lovesick woman in the short film "Symphony in Black" with Duke Ellington.

1933 — The Civilian Conservation Corps: Green Money

On April 5, 1933, President Franklin Roosevelt establishes the Civilian Conservation Corps (CCC), a federal organization that puts thousands of Americans to work on environmental projects. The CCC enrolls mostly young, unskilled and unemployed men between the ages of 18 and 25. Along with room and board at a work camp, each man earns $30 a month, the bulk of which must be sent home to support his family. CCC employees fight forest fires, plant trees, clear roads, re-seed grazing lands and implement soil-erosion controls. They also build wildlife refuges and water storage basins. Employees who are illiterate can learn to read and write while serving in the CCC. Women are prohibited from working in the program.

This Page:
These snapshots show examples of the Depression-era "house dress," a cotton or broadcloth garment that featured handy pockets, no-fuss durability and a loose fit.

1933 — Chicago Hosts the World's Fair

Built along the shores of Lake Michigan on more than 400 acres of land, the Century of Progress Exposition opens on May 27, 1933. The action sprawls between the newly-completed Adler Planetarium (1930) to 37th Street and is operated by using cheap labor to keep costs low. Attractions include gleaming Art Deco buildings, futuristic science exhibits, a carnival midway, a sky tram ride and the scandalous fan dancer Sally Rand. Millions of people scrape up the 50 cent admission fee and head to the fair, which in addition to commemorating Chicago's past, serves as a symbol of hope during the depths Great Depression. The expo runs from May to November and returns for an encore in the summer of 1934.

1933 — Thank God That's Over … How About a Beer?

A failed experiment in forced morality comes to an end when the 21st Amendment to the Constitution is passed on December 5, 1933. It repeals the 18th Amendment — also known as the Volstead Act — which had ushered in Prohibition in 1919 and made the manufacture, distribution and sale of alcoholic beverages illegal. Crime rates soared under Prohibition as gangsters took advantage of the immensely profitable black market for alcohol. After learning that enforcement of a no-booze policy is virtually impossible, the federal government gives up. Saloons re-open, the liquor flows freely and everybody ties one on.

1934 — FDR's Missus Becomes a Power in Her Own Right

As First Lady of the United States, Eleanor Roosevelt breaks new ground. Not only does she travel on her husband's behalf due to his limited mobility, she shares her findings and recommendations with the president. Through Eleanor's updates, FDR is kept apprised of how average Americans are coping with Depression-era poverty. He values her analyses and her solutions as well. Eleanor holds her own press conferences and limits access to female reporters only. She writes a daily syndicated newspaper column called "My Day," hosts frequent radio programs and gives public lectures. Eleanor often discusses controversial topics (birth control, workers rights) as a means of stimulating public debate.

1934 — Bonnie Parker: Your Typical Cigar-Smoking Gun Moll

Bonnie Parker and her companion, Clyde Champion Barrow, are shot to death by law enforcement officers in Sailes, Bienville Parish, Louisiana, on May 23, 1934. At the time of the ambush, Bonnie and Clyde are wanted for 13 murders, kidnapping, vehicle theft, and a string of robberies and burglaries. Their crime spree and ensuing manhunt had kept the nation riveted. Americans viewed Bonnie, 23, and Clyde, 25, as rebels who had

This Page:
Above: Snapshot, Century of Progress, Chicago, 1934.
Below: Snapshot, well-dressed girl with dog on a leash, 1934.

Opposite Page:
Top: Frontier "salloon" patrons, 1930s.
Left: Motorcycle mama, 1938.
Right: Woman with moonshine jug, 1930s.

Above:
Studio portrait, 1930s.

Below:
Studio portrait, 1930s.

embraced a glamorous outlaw lifestyle — complete with premarital sex — and gone completely astray. Unbeknownst to many, when she died, Parker was actually married to another man named Roy Thornton, who was serving time in prison for bank robbery.

1934 — FDR Signs the Securities Exchange Act

On June 6, 1934, President Franklin Roosevelt establishes the U.S. Securities and Exchange Commission (SEC). The independent government agency is created to protect investors and is the first federal regulator of securities markets. The SEC promotes full public disclosure and monitors corporate takeovers. It is also designed to prevent investors from falling victim to fraudulent or manipulative market practices.

1934 — Girl Scout Cookies: Baking Up A Revenue Stream

While industrious Girl Scouts and their mothers were baking cookies in their family kitchens as far back as 1917, it isn't until 1934 that the sweet treats become mass produced. In Philadelphia, a group of Girl Scouts who are working on their cooking badges actually get the ball rolling in 1933. They hold public baking demonstrations on new gas ranges that are showcased in the windows of the Philadelphia Gas Works. The publicity stunt works wonders and cookie sales tick upward — even at 23 cents per box. In 1934, the Philadelphia Girl Scouts hire the Keebler Baking Company to whip up their trefoil-shaped sugar cookies so they can better focus on marketing, public relations, and financing various troop activities.

1934 — Arthurdale: Eleanor's Haven for the Poor

Finding that portions of West Virginia are among the areas hardest hit by the Great Depression, Eleanor Roosevelt creates Arthurdale, a government-sponsored residential community for 165 impoverished families. Under the terms of a 30-year-loan, each family receives a small house, a parcel of land and some livestock with which to start fresh. When the project runs into cash-flow problems, Eleanor asks her wealthy friends to help finance it and uses her own personal income to run it.

1934 — Great Island Views, Free Rent … And No Escape

The first federal prisoners classified as "most dangerous" arrive at Alcatraz Federal Penitentiary on August 11, 1934. The high-security prison becomes known as "The Rock" due to its terrain and isolated location, more than a mile offshore in San Francisco Bay. Some of the country's most notorious criminals do time at Alcatraz. Among them are Al Capone; Doc Barker (of the Ma Barker Gang); George "Machine Gun" Kelly; Robert "Birdman of Alcatraz" Stroud; and Alvin "Creepy" Karpis.

1934 — Bette Davis Hits Her Stride in "Of Human Bondage"

After more than 20 film roles, actress Bette Davis earns her first critical acclaim when she plays the spiteful waitress Mildred Rogers in the RKO Radio Pictures drama "Of Human Bondage." An adaptation of W. Somerset Maugham's novel, the Pre-Code film allows Davis to show her range as an actress by being downright cold, cruel and calculating — traits that are simply not deemed appropriate for a lady, regardless of her social station.

1935 — Under FDR, Three Sweeping Reform Programs Are Born

- Works Progress Administration: Changes the face of America forever by building or rebuilding 2,500 hospitals; 6,000 public schools; 10,000 airport landing fields and thousands of roads coast-to-coast. Gives support to artists, writers and musicians and brings cultural offerings to underserved rural areas. Publishes printed guides to all 48 states; finances mural paintings on public buildings.
- National Youth Administration: Provides training for young people, ages 16 to 25, who are not in school and are out of work.
- Rural Electrification Administration: Brings electricity to the nation's rural areas. Farmers are urged to create electricity cooperative companies, which are then funded through low-interest loans. New distribution facilities and power lines make it possible for farms to have electric appliances and equipment, running water and radios.

1935 — A Thoroughly Modern Race Riot

When a mixed-race Puerto Rican teenage boy steals a penknife from a dime store in the New York borough of Harlem on March 19, 1935, his small misdeed triggers a devastating chain of events. Years of unemployment, economic hardship and police brutality help fuel a rumor that the boy had been beaten while in police custody. (The story is untrue.) That evening, during a protest outside the store, a rock is thrown through the window. Protesters destroy not only the dime store, but white-owned properties throughout the community. The upheaval becomes known as the first "modern" race riot in Harlem, because it is committed primarily against property rather than against people.

1935 — Black Sunday and The Dust Bowl

Chaos blankets the overplowed Great Plains region when, on Sunday, April 14, 1935, the worst "black blizzard" occurs. The trouble begins when a cold front from Canada meets warm air over the Dakotas and temperatures fall more than 30 degrees in a few hours. The resulting winds create a dust cloud hundreds of miles wide and thousands of feet high. As the skies turn black,

Above:
Snapshot, woman, girl and chickens, posing in flower garden, 1930s.

Below:
Snapshot, women posing on sidewalk in work jackets and overalls, 1930s.

Above:
Snapshot, woman and baby, dated 1935.

Below:
Snapshot, woman and baby, 1930s.

drivers take refuge in their cars. Others seek shelter in barns, cellars and even under their beds. The storm drags on for hours, and when it finally subsides, thousands of tons of dried-out topsoil is gone and sediment is found as far away as the East Coast of the United States. In the aftermath, the term "Dust Bowl" enters the nation's vocabulary.

1935 — Starting the Cleanup

On April 27, 1935, Congress declares soil erosion "a national menace" and establishes the Soil Conservation Service in the Department of Agriculture. The SCS develops conservation efforts and new programs to help restore the farmland in the drought region. Landowners are taught how to rotate crops and use techniques such as contour plowing and terracing to prevent irreparable damage to the topsoil.

1935 — Labor Finally Gets a Seat at the Table

The Wagner Act establishes official protection for workers' and unions' rights when President Franklin Roosevelt signs it into law on July 5, 1935. This piece of legislation creates the National Labor Relations Board (NLRB), which protects workers' ability to organize, bargain collectively and strike. Coming on the heels of decades of American labor protests, hardscrabble wages and grotesquely unsafe working conditions, The Wagner Act makes the federal government a guiding force and an arbitrator in employer-employee disputes.

1935 — Social Security: Caring for Widows, Orphans and Elderly

Perhaps the most important social shift occurs under President Franklin Roosevelt's New Deal when he signs The Social Security Act on August 14, 1935. It includes provisions for dependent women and children and establishes a social insurance program designed to pay older workers, age 65 and up, a continuing income after retirement. Under the act, Social Security will begin payouts to retirees within two years. Workers begin contributing into the system in 1937, at a rate of 2 percent of the first $3,000 in earnings, half paid by the employee and half paid by the employer.

1935 — FDR Decides That Preservation Is a Necessity

President Franklin Roosevelt ensures that the nation's historic buildings, objects and landmarks will be protected when he signs the Historic Sites Act on August 21, 1935. The act allows the Secretary of the Interior to determine how to best curate and preserve archaeological sites, significant buildings or structures — as well as plans, photographs and data pertaining to them — in order to safeguard the nation's history. The act also enumerates a wide range of powers and responsibilities for the National Park Service.

1935 — The Hoover Dam: A Hard Hat Zone in the Desert

American laborers exceed all expectations when the Hoover Dam is dedicated on September 30, 1935 — two years ahead of schedule and under budget. Located in the Black Canyon, 30 miles outside of Las Vegas, Nevada, the dam provides flood control, irrigation, drinking water and electricity to the American Southwest. A consortium of six construction companies employed 5,000 men for the project, paying them an average of $1 an hour. (Temperatures on the job site average 119 degrees.) After the Colorado River is diverted and six million tons of concrete are poured, the completed Hoover Dam stands 726 feet high and forms Lake Mead, the largest reservoir in the United States. Final price tag: $49 million.

1935 — Mary McLeod Bethune Joins FDR's Brain Trust

African-American educator and philanthropist Mary McLeod Bethune becomes director of the Office of Minority Affairs of the National Youth Administration (NYA) in 1935. She serves as a trusted advisor to President Franklin Roosevelt on issues relating to the education, employment and the civil rights of African-Americans. As one of 17 children born to two former slaves, Bethune's own education had begun in a one-room schoolhouse. Her drive to excel earned her mentors, benefactors and a college scholarship. Originally planning to become a missionary, Bethune instead founded a private school for African-American girls in Daytona Beach, Florida, and dedicated her life to educating others.

1936 — Baby Takes a Bow and Gets a Big Paycheck

On February 27, 1936, child mega-star Shirley Temple snags a new contract from 20th Century Fox that will pay her $50,000 per film. Though she is only seven years old, the curly-haired Temple is the nation's top box-office draw. Her cheerful persona and genuine talent act as a balm on America's injured psyche during the bleakest years of the Great Depression.

1936 — Thank You, Gertrude!

Denver businesswoman Gertrude Tenderich makes a savvy investment in 1936 when she buys the patent for the "applicator tampon" that Dr. Earle Haas invented in 1929. Tenderich wastes no time in founding the Tampax Sales Corporation, where she serves as president. By July, she is promoting her product directly to American women via national magazines. Early ads tout the tampon by promising that: "Belts, pins and pads are, of course, eliminated. In fact, the wearer is completely unconscious of its presence." The newfangled Tampax tampon allows women to live happier, more active lives — doing things like swimming, dancing and riding horses with carefree abandon. We love Gertrude.

Above:
Snapshot, woman seated in the parlor holding a book, 1930s.

Below:
Snapshot, bathing beauty, 1930s.

Above:
Snapshot, women playing a game, 1930s.

Below:
Snapshot, smiling older woman holding yawning infant, 1930s.

1936 — FDR Praises Americans for Rallying and Conquering Fear

Having received the Democratic Party's nomination for the 1936 presidential election, President Franklin Roosevelt promises to continue leading the country in its recovery efforts. On June 27, 1936, he tells the delegates gathered for the Democratic National Convention in Philadelphia: "There is a mysterious cycle in human events. To some generations, much is given. Of other generations much is expected. This generation of Americans has a rendezvous with destiny."

1936 — Author Margaret Mitchell Gives a Damn

When a dismissive friend says that she'll never finish her nine-year-old manuscript, Atlanta journalist Margaret Mitchell takes offense and puts the pedal to the metal. She rewrites and polishes her thousands of pages of copy and submits it to Macmillan Publishing. The end result is Mitchell's mega-novel "Gone With the Wind," which chronicles the demise of the Old South during and after the Civil War. On June 30, 1936, GWTW is published and Scarlett O'Hara becomes a household name. Fiddle-dee-dee!

1936 — Rx Birth Control Legalized in Landmark Case

A package sent from Japan and seized by U.S. Customs becomes the pivot point in America's birth control debate. (Spoiler alert: It contained 120 rubber pessaries — also known as Japanese diaphragms — and was confiscated by authorities.) On December 7, 1936, a U.S. Federal Court rules in *United States v. One Package* that the 1873 Comstock Law's definition of obscenity does not apply to birth control. The Comstock Law was meant to stop trade in "obscene literature" and "immoral articles" and was used to prosecute those who distributed information or devices used for contraception. The court case, which was orchestrated by Margaret Sanger, secured a legal foundation of reproductive rights.

1936 — "The Women" Takes Aim at the Lush Life

After having been an active suffragette and the associate editor of *Vanity Fair* magazine, Clare Boothe Luce has a smash hit with her play, "The Women," which opens on Broadway on December 26, 1936. The play skewers the lives of Manhattan socialites and the gossip that complicates their relationships. An all-female cast spends considerable time discussing and analyzing the men in their lives (and their pursuits thereof), but the male characters never appear onstage.

1937 — The Shelterbelt Project Takes Root

President Franklin Roosevelt makes his struggling Shelterbelt Project an official part of the Works Progress Administration (WPA) in order to secure its funding. The project had been launched in 1934 in response to the devastation in the Dust Bowl region, but Congress is slow to finance it in the midst of the Great Depression. The Shelterbelt Project calls for large-scale planting of trees across the Great Plains, from Canada to Texas, to protect the land from soil erosion. Its goal is to bring thousands of native trees, such as red cedar and green ash, to the region to reduce wind velocity and lessen moisture evaporation.

1937 — The Hindenburg Disaster

On May 6, 1937, the 804-foot luxury German airship Hindenburg explodes into a mass of flames while attempting to dock at Lakehurst, New Jersey. The hydrogen gas-filled zeppelin had just completed a much-publicized trans-Atlantic flight and the media coverage is considerable. Newsreel photographers capture the entire disaster. WLS radio reporter Herbert Morrison's live eyewitness coverage includes his chilling exclamation, "Oh, the humanity!" The tragedy claims 36 lives: 13 passengers, 22 crewmen and one crew member on the ground.

1937 — Zora Neal Hurston Pens a Classic

In her novel, "Their Eyes Were Watching God," author Zora Neal Hurston tells it like it is. She weaves the action-packed life story of Janie Crawford, an African-American woman who marries three times in a search for love and her own identity. The book is poorly received upon publication and even condemned by some of the male writers who gained prominence during the

Above:
Snapshot, woman in stylish, wide-legged trousers, posing with dog, late 1930s.

Below:
Woman seated on the dock, late 1930s.

Above:
Informal studio portrait, late 1930s.

Below:
Snapshot, stamped August 1937.

Harlem Renaissance. However, after her death, Hurston's book comes to be revered as a masterpiece and a cornerstone of African-American literature.

1937 — The Golden Gate Bridge: An Architectural Marvel

After five years of construction in storms, fog and strong tides, San Francisco's 4,200-foot-long Golden Gate Bridge opens for "Pedestrian Day" on May 27, 1937. Thousands of walkers explore the new suspension bridge, which now connects San Francisco and Marin County. The bridge features a distinctive orange color, which was chosen for its resistance to rust and fading, as well as its aesthetic quality. The next morning, the structure opens to vehicular traffic for the first time.

1937 — The Mystery and Legend of Amelia Earhart

American aviation pioneer Amelia Earhart disappears over the Pacific Ocean while attempting to circumnavigate the globe on July 2, 1937. The trouble occurs on the final and most dangerous leg of the 29,000-mile journey. While piloting a Lockheed Model 10-E Electra, Earhart and her navigator, Fred Noonan, lose their bearings after leaving Lae, New Guinea. During this portion of the flight, the U.S. Coast Guard cutter Itasca is in sporadic radio contact with Earhart. As she approaches Howland Island, she sends messages saying she is lost and running out of fuel. The Itasca responds with multiple radio transmissions, but Earhart cannot hear them. When contact with the plane ceases, a massive sea and air rescue is launched, but no trace of Earhart or Noonan is ever found.

1937 — The First Disney Princess Cleans House in Technicolor

Walt Disney Productions premieres "Snow White and the Seven Dwarves" on December 21, 1937 at the Carthay Circle Theater in Los Angeles. Creating the very first full-length, cel-animated movie is a huge gamble for Disney. Luckily, the magic spell takes hold and the fairytale romance pays off big, earning $8 million during its initial box office run. The film sets the standard for the company's future animated efforts. Snow White herself proves that domesticity can be somewhat isolating, even if your nice bosses own a diamond mine, and that poison apples are no joke.

1938 — Minimum Wage and OT Become the Norm

Working folks get a boost when on June 25, 1938, the Fair Labor Standards Act (FLSA) becomes the law of the land as part of President Franklin Roosevelt's New Deal. The FLSA sets nationwide standards for employees of organizations engaged in interstate commerce, operations of a certain size, and public agencies. The act establishes the first minimum wage (25 cents per hour) and limits the work week to 44 hours. The FLSA also formalizes

the concept "time-and-a-half" pay for overtime work. Most significantly, the act bans child labor, meaning the children under age 14 can no longer legally work, though exceptions are made for agricultural jobs and small family-run businesses.

This Page:
Above: Professional group portrait, 1937.
Below: Snapshot, "Mary & Me," 1930s.

1938 — Pearl S. Buck: A Nobel Laureate at Age 46

West Virginia-born author Pearl S. Buck receives the Nobel Prize for Literature in 1938, making her the first American woman to win the honor. Buck had been raised in China by missionary parents. She wove her experiences and observations into her first novel, "East Wind, West Wind," which was published in 1930. It was followed by "The Good Earth" (1931), "Sons" (1932), and "A House Divided" (1935), a trilogy about the Wang family and their struggles to survive.

1938 — I Can See Clearly Now, the Glare is Gone

After earning her Ph.D. in physics from the University of Cambridge, Katharine Burr Blodgett becomes the first female scientist to work at the General Electric Laboratory. Blodgett's research in physics and chemistry result in her invention of "invisible" or non-reflective glass. Drawing inspiration from the way oil reflects light off of water and how soap bubbles change color based on their thickness, Blodgett creates the world's first

Above:
Snapshot, female boat passengers, 1930s.

Below:
Snapshot, "Easter Sunday, Iowa, 1938."

transparent glass. Her process is patented in 1938 and is used to limit distortion in eyeglasses, microscopes, telescopes, cameras and projectors.

1938 — Ella Fitzgerald: "The First Lady of Song"

At the tender age of 21, jazz vocalist Ella Fitzgerald records a unique version of the nursery rhyme "A-Tisket, A-Tasket." Fitzgerald is a staple at Harlem's Savoy Ballroom, but it's this breakthrough recording — made with the Chick Webb Orchestra — that cements her national fame. The record sells one million copies and hits No. 1 on "Your Hit Parade."

1938 — "War of the Worlds" Scares the Bejeezus Out of Everyone

Under the category of "It seemed like a good idea at the time ..." Orson Welles and the Mercury Theatre players present a radio adaptation of H.G. Wells' novel, "The War of the Worlds" on October 30, 1938. The program, which is broadcast nationwide on CBS, includes fake news bulletins that depict a Martian invasion of the Earth. The fictional conflict is centered on the New Jersey town of Grover's Mill. The acting is so top-notch and the sound effects are so realistic that panic ensues across the country. Highways in New Jersey are jammed as thousands try to flee from the Martians.

1938 — Baby Snooks Is On the Air!

Ziegfeld Follies star Fannie Brice brings one of her most popular characters, the toddler Baby Snooks, to the masses when she launches her new radio

Cabin at Gatlinburg - Tenn. 9-27-39

career in November 1938. In response to rampant anti-Semitism in the United States and Europe, Brice is trying to distance herself from the Yiddish characters (and accents) she made famous while working on the stage with Ziegfeld. Fifteen years earlier, with a movie career in her sights, Brice had also opted to have plastic surgery to achieve a less ethnic appearance. This decision prompted the writer Dorothy Parker to quip that Brice had "cut off her nose to spite her race."

1939 — Hooray for Hollywood!

The studio system cranks out some stellar movies in 1939 including the Best Picture Oscar winner, "Gone With the Wind." Imagine following Dorothy down the yellow brick road in "The Wizard of Oz;" watching Jimmy Stewart tackle politics in "Mr. Smith Goes to Washington;" weeping over Bette Davis' performance in "Dark Victory;" and rooting for newcomer John Wayne in "Stagecoach" — all in the same year. Quality scripts, excellent acting and newfangled visuals make for tremendous ticket sales. A little more than 10 years after the debut of "talkies," motion pictures have reached a new level of sophistication and artistry.

1939 — Marian Anderson Gives a Concert in Washington, D.C.

Despite being a huge box-office draw, African-American contralto Marian Anderson is rebuffed when her managers try to book her for a performance at Constitution Hall in Washington, D.C. The Daughters of the American

Above:
Snapshot, woman outside "Cabin at Gatlinburg, Tenn., 9-27-39."

Below:
Snapshot, aspiring movie star, 1930s.

Above:
Snapshot, woman with fur stole, 1930s.

Below:
Studio portrait, late 1930s.

Revolution, who own the hall, deny the request and act in keeping with segregationist policies of the day. In response, Eleanor Roosevelt publicly resigns from the D.A.R. Then, she arranges for Anderson to give a concert on the steps of the Lincoln Memorial. Anderson does so on Easter Sunday, April 9, 1939. Wrapped in a mink coat and accompanied by a lone pianist, Anderson stands before a bank of radio microphones and an audience of 75,000. When she launches her 25-minute concert with a rendition of "My Country 'Tis of Thee," she makes American history.

1939 — Karen Horney Kicks Penis Envy to the Curb

After emigrating to the United States in 1932, German psychoanalyst Karen Horney heads to Brooklyn. She settles in a large, Jewish community — home to many refugees from Nazi Germany — and begins a period of academic work that makes her a pioneer in the discipline of feminine psychiatry. In 1939, Horney publishes her second book, "New Ways in Psychoanalysis." In it, she challenges Freudianism by suggesting that penis envy is a phallic fallacy. (No pun intended.) Horney goes one step further by saying the childbirth and breastfeeding are so awesome that men may suffer from "womb envy." She also concludes that women are intellectually superior to men, and therefore, need to be productive and self-actualized.

1939 — Billie Holiday Speaks Up for Her "Pop" in Song

In protest of racism and the practice of lynching that is widespread in the Southern states, on April 20, 1939, jazz chanteuse Billie Holiday records "Strange Fruit" for Commodore Records. When Holiday goes on to perform the song live at Cafe Society in Greenwich Village in New York, she does so with her father in mind. (He died at age 39 after being denied medical treatment in Texas at a "whites only" hospital.) Holiday makes the song part of her permanent repertoire, "Not only because people ask for it, but because 20 years after Pop died, the things that killed him are still happening in the South."

1939 — World's Fair Offers a Glimpse of the Future

Sprawling across 1,200 acres in the borough of Queens, the World's Fair opens on April 30, 1939. The site, which had previously been an ash dump, is transformed to showcase the latest developments in transportation, the arts, government and technology. FM radio, robotics, the fax machine and fluorescent lighting are all introduced at the fair. President Franklin Roosevelt's opening speech is broadcast on the new medium of television to 200 black-and-white TV sets scattered across the New York metropolitan area. Aquatic performances, girlie shows, exotic animals, amusement park rides and "Democracity," a model of a utopian city of the future, are among the attractions. Two iconic structures — Trylon and Perisphere — symbolize the fair and its theme: "Dawn of a New Day." More than 44 million people attend the fair prior to its closure on October 27, 1940.

1939 — Grandma Moses' Art Exhibited at the MOMA

Anna Mary Robertson Moses, a 78-year-old grandmother displays several of her amateur paintings in a drugstore window near her home in upstate New York in 1938. A traveling NYC art dealer finds her primitive style of depicting folk tales and childhood memories beguiling. He buys all the paintings in the store, plus a few more from her stash at home. Moses' paintings of quilting bees, picket fences, horse-drawn carriages and old-fashioned farm life appeal to the avant-garde in the city. Her works are shown at the Museum of Modern Art in New York the following year.

1939 — Germany Invades Poland

Adolph Hitler unleashes his "*blitzkrieg*" (lightning war) strategy when German forces invade Poland on September 1, 1939. The German Luftwaffe (air force) drops bombs to destroy Poland's defense capabilities and infrastructure and Hitler's ground troops follow up with a massive invasion. Once the borders are overrun, the Germans advance on Warsaw, the capital city. This aggression begins World War II and Hitler's ethnic cleansing efforts to eliminate all those who oppose his Nazi ideology.

1939 — Mother Nature Comes Through for the Heartland

After nearly a decade of drought, the Great Plains states finally start to receive substantial rain in the autumn of 1939. The dust storms that had smothered vegetation and animals alike subside. While some people blame the environmental disaster on the wrath of God, the drought appears to be a product of natural climate fluctuation. The combination of new techniques in farming and conservation — along with the increased rainfall — rejuvenate the land and wheat is plentiful once again. The area recovers just in time to go to war.

Above:
Snapshot, Holy Family High School graduate, 1938.

Below:
Snapshot, rural landscape, 1930s.

Fashion Footnotes from Photos of the 1930s

The 1930s — "The Great Depression"

Following the stock market crash of 1929, America plunges into an era defined by mass unemployment, anxiety and need. The wealthy continue living large, while average families struggle to get by on what little they do have. Hollywood films showcase glamour, adventure and comedy, making the local theater a nice place to visit to escape reality for a few hours.

Fashion trends from the decade include:

- People are feeling contrite and frightened; propriety, modesty, rules and good behavior are embraced. The boyish fashion looks of the 1920s are abandoned in the face of social upheaval.
- Dominant Fashion Idea #1: Femininity returns in the form of sleek, slinky dresses that feature a natural waistline.
- Dominant Fashion Idea #2: Very low hemlines, dainty little shoes.
- Dominant Fashion Idea #3: Small, soft prints are popular for casual, everyday dresses. Polka dots spread like a fashion rash; they're even featured in men's accessories.
- Hats and gloves are commonplace; the dreaded corset comes back.
- The poor are miserable, but the rich show off their prosperity with swanky evening wear and furs.
- Women's hairstyles are soft and wavy.
- Eyebrows are thin and arched; false eyelashes, lilac eyeshadow and a glossy red lip are makeup trends.
- The first backless dresses appear in elegant evening fashions.
- Wealthy women embrace French Riviera-inspired resort wear such as palazzo pants and big straw hats.
- Africa becomes a fashion influence; leopard and cheetah prints pop up in women's clothing and accessories.
- Outlaw Bonnie Parker popularizes the beret-and-scarf combo.
- Ladies' fashion icons: Movie stars Jean Harlow, Greta Garbo and Marlene Dietrich, along with jetsetter Wallis Simpson

Above:
Studio portrait, 1930s.

Opposite Page:
Studio portrait, dated 1938.

Below:
Snapshot, "Waiting for a cab," late 1930s.

1940s: World War II, Rations and Rosie the Riveter

"A woman is like a tea bag — you can't tell how strong she is until you put her in hot water."

— *Eleanor Roosevelt (1884-1962), First Lady of the United States and social advocate*

In a country where older citizens can still recall the horrors of World War I and where economic recovery is stalling, most Americans favor isolationism. They see no compelling reason to engage in another overseas military conflict. All that changes on December 7, 1941 when hundreds of Japanese fighter planes attack the American naval base at Pearl Harbor in Hawaii. The following day, President Franklin D. Roosevelt asks Congress to declare war on Japan.

As the men leave to serve in the military during World War II, a robust government campaign is launched to convince American women to join the civilian workforces. The ladies do not disappoint. They roll up their sleeves and punch in at steel plants, shipyards and lumber mills — and do so for reduced wages. Others knit socks for soldiers and organize rubber, metal and paper drives. When kitchen staples such as sugar, meat and canned goods are in short supply due to rationing, American women stretch what little they do have in order to prepare food for their families. Gasoline is also rationed, further restricting their activities and mobility.

Fashion during the war becomes utilitarian and uniforms abound. Women "make do" by taking men's old civilian suits and tailoring them in order to design skirt-and-jacket combos they can wear themselves. Radio is a lifeline for Americans as the cheapest form of entertainment. It is also used to bolster the country's mood and its support for the Allied forces. Big band music, situation comedies, soap operas, variety shows and dramatic serial programs fill the airwaves.

In 1945, the new American president, Harry S. Truman, makes the controversial and world-changing decision to drop atomic bombs on the Japanese cities of Hiroshima and Nagasaki; casualties exceed 120,000.

When the war finally ends, Americans turn their attention to home, hearth and family. A "Baby Boom" ensues, ushering in an era of prosperity, consumerism, social conservatism — all of which takes place amid a pervasive Cold War-related anxiety.

Above:
Snapshot, woman on staircase, 1940s.

Below:
Snapshot, woman with two sailors, 1940s.

Previous Spread:
Left: Snapshot, soldier and family, 1940s.
Right: Professional portrait, captioned on back: PFC Florence Stewart, Fort Riley, Kansas, February 1944.

1940 — Hattie McDaniel Breaks the Barrier

Her masterful performance as Mammy in "Gone With the Wind" earns Hattie McDaniel the Academy Award for Best Supporting Actress in 1940. She becomes the first African-American to win an Oscar. Due to the segregationist attitudes of the time, none of GWTW's African-American actors are allowed to attend the film's 1939 premiere at the Loew's Grand Theatre on Peachtree Street in Atlanta, Georgia. This includes McDaniel.

1941 — Focusing on Lange and Bourke-White

Two of the most groundbreaking and prolific American photojournalists, Dorothea Lange and Margaret Bourke-White, are formally honored for their work in the early 1940s. Dorothea Lange becomes the first woman to be awarded a Guggenheim Fellowship in 1941, and Margaret Bourke-White becomes the first female war correspondent the following year, as the official photographer for the U.S. Air Force.

1941 — Wonder Woman Kicks Ass

Superhuman strength and speed are great, but it's the accessories — the bulletproof bracelets, the tiara and the Golden Lasso of Truth — that really make Wonder Woman an unforgettable gal. In October 1941, she makes her DC Comics debut and gives female patriotism a new look as she wages war against Axis villains. With her Amazonian heritage and a birth story based on Greek mythology (hence the superpowers), Wonder Woman shreds the stereotype of the damsel in distress.

1941 — Remember Pearl Harbor

At 7:55 a.m., on December 7, 1941, hundreds of Japanese fighter planes attack the U.S. Pacific Fleet at Pearl Harbor, Hawaii. The fleet is destroyed and more than 2,400 Americans (including civilians) perish and an estimated 1,000 more are wounded. Almost half the fatalities occur on the U.S.S. Arizona, which is hit several times and sinks in a fiery explosion. A total of 19 U.S. ships are destroyed or damaged. The early morning attack unites outraged Americans, many of whom had previously favored isolationism. When President Franklin D. Roosevelt addresses Congress the next day to ask for a declaration of war against Japan, he calls December 7, "a date which will live in infamy." The United States officially enters World War II.

1941 — Women in the U.S. Armed Forces

During World War II, some 350,000 women serve in the U.S. Armed Forces, both at home and abroad. They join the Women's Army Auxiliary Corps (WAC); the civilian Women Airforce Service Pilots (WASP); the

Women Accepted for Volunteer Military Services (WAVES) and a branch of the Coast Guard (SPARS). The majority of the women serve as typists and clerks who keep the military's bureaucratic wheels turning. A smaller number work in medical jobs that bring them close to the front lines.

This Page:
Above, Left: Studio portrait, 1940s.
Above: Snapshot, three ladies wearing summer "day dresses," 1940s.
Below: Snapshot, dated "1942."

1941 — Those Andrews Sisters Can Really Swing!

Talk about a triple threat! Patty, Maxene and LaVerne Andrews deliver an optimistic message of hope and American allegiance during the war years, becoming one of the most successful girl groups of all time along the way. With their pitch-perfect harmonies in sync, the sisters appear in Hollywood movies, on radio broadcasts and in nightclubs all over the country. They also perform in USO touring shows, entertaining the troops with numbers like "Boogie Woogie Bugle Boy;" "Don't Sit Under the Apple Tree (With Anyone Else But Me);" and the "Beer Barrel Polka."

1942 — Introducing Planned Parenthood

In the interest of refining its marketing strategy, the American Birth Control League changes its name to the Planned Parenthood Federation of America in 1942. Birth control pioneer Margaret Sanger — who has been on the front lines of the struggle for decades — is not pleased. (She opened the first birth control clinic in the United States in 1916 in the New York City borough of Brooklyn and was arrested for doing so.) However, the change is adopted because the league members believe that the new name has a positive connotation and will be more acceptable to Americans in general.

Above:
Studio portrait, created at Fusaki Studio, 1747 Buchanan St., San Francisco, 1940s.

Below and Opposite Page:
Snapshots, women in uniforms, 1940s.

1942 — Executive Order 9066: Japanese Internment Camps

The internment of Japanese Americans in the United States during World War II represents the forced relocation and incarceration in camps of more than 120,000 people of Japanese descent. More than 60 percent of these adults and children are American citizens who live on the Pacific Coast. The camps, situated in extremely desolate areas in the Western states, are authorized by President Franklin D. Roosevelt on February 19, 1942 when he signs Executive Order 9066. The internment process is instituted to deter alleged Japanese spies after the attack on Pearl Harbor.

1942 — Hedy Lamarr's "Secret Communication System"

Proving that she is more than just a pretty face, Hollywood actress Hedy Lamarr teams up with her friend George Antheil, a composer and pianist, to bolster the war effort. Lamarr envisions a frequency-hopping signal that cannot be tracked or jammed, which would increase the efficacy of the U.S. Navy's radio-controlled torpedoes. Antheil executes Lamarr's idea by using a miniature player-piano mechanism. On August 11, 1942, Lamarr and Antheil receive U.S. Patent 2,292,387 for their invention. (While the technology proves too difficult to implement and is not used during World War II, decades later it becomes the foundation for wireless telecommunications technologies such as Bluetooth, Wi-Fi and GPS.)

1943 — Girls Just Wanna Run Bases

The All-American Girls Professional Baseball League becomes the first professional baseball league for female players. The league is the brainchild of chewing gum mogul Philip K. Wrigley, who fears that the war will obliterate Major League Baseball — and the Chicago Cubs franchise he happens to own. (The draft had already caused many minor league teams to disband.) During its existence, more than 600 women play in the AAGPBL. Femininity is a priority on and off the field. Players are given makeup kits and must attend evening charm school classes. The most successful team, the Rockford Peaches, wins the league championship four times.

1943 — The Pentagon Provides a Strong Center

On January 15, 1943, the Pentagon is completed after 16 months of round-the-clock construction. Located in Arlington, Virginia, across the Potomac River from Washington, D.C., the massive five-sided structure is designed so that the U.S. War Department's 24,000 workers can be housed in a central headquarters. Military personnel from 17 different buildings in the Washington area begin moving into the Pentagon. The structure is so large that messengers can travel between departments on roller skates or bicycles, using the building's internal concrete ramps as thoroughfares.

1943 — Warsaw Ghetto Uprising

On Passover Eve, April 19, 1943, German troops and police descend upon the ghetto in Warsaw, Poland, intent on relocating its residents. The Jews who live in the ghetto had watched for months as their family, friends and neighbors were deported in waves, having allegedly been sent to labor camps. However, by 1942, word travels back to ghetto residents that the process actually ends in mass extermination at German concentration camps. Armed with smuggled and homemade weapons, the Jewish residents of the ghetto launch an uprising that lasts until May 16, when the Great Synagogue of Warsaw is detonated. The ghetto is left in ruins and those who remain are deported nonetheless, but the resistance effort becomes legendary.

1943 — A Perfect Storm Fuels Detroit Race Riot

As the military buildup escalates, the automotive industry in Detroit is converted to produce vehicles for the war effort. Between 1941 and 1943, thousands of African-American and white migrants leave the southern United States in search of high-paying factory jobs in Detroit. Instead, they find a crushing housing shortage and resentment on the part of the city's already established residents. To add to the tension, during the prosperity

Ration Stamps for Shopping:
On August 28, 1941, President Roosevelt's Executive Order 8875 creates the Office of Price Administration (OPA); its function is to place a ceiling on prices of most goods, and to limit consumption by rationing.

True Story:
In 1943, when the ration stamps shown below were issued, my mother was the 13-year-old recipient. Every American was entitled to a series of ration books for buying restricted items. Somehow, my mother lost this particular book and her parents punished her for doing so. When she found it again weeks later, she hid it. Her parents continued to frantically search for the book and punished her again when it didn't turn up! My mother gave me these stamps in the 1990s. She said she always knew she should save them for her children to see one day. She never told her parents.

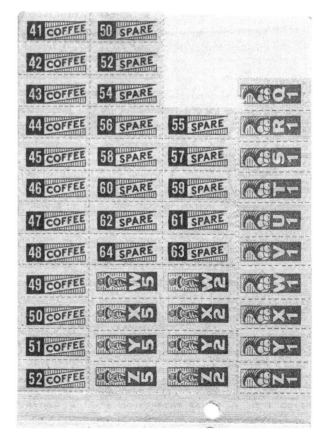

This Page:
Left: Photobooth portrait, woman in uniform, inscribed "Hasta la Vista, Mac."

Right: Snapshot, military canteen workers, 1940s. (During the war, American women volunteer to staff military canteens in their hometowns, many of which operate near small railroad depots. They dispense free coffee, box lunches, magazines, candy, doughnuts and cigarettes to any man or woman in uniform.)

Below: Snapshot, two women pose with a young sailor near the family's home, 1940s.

of the 1920s, the Ku Klux Klan had branched out to the Midwest and had established an active presence in Michigan. Overcrowding, scarce resources and unchecked racism spark a riot that begins on June 20, 1943 and lasts until June 22, when 6,000 federal troops arrive to shut it down.

1943 — Benito is Finito

Time's up for Benito Mussolini, the fascist dictator of Italy, on July 25, 1943. After leaving a meeting with King Vittorio Emanuele, Mussolini is arrested by the royal police. The plans for Mussolini's removal had long been in the works — and for General Pietro Badoglio to assume the role of prime minister — as it is apparent that the Allies are going to win the war. Mussolini resigns and is imprisoned. Adolph Hitler later orchestrates Mussolini's escape and installs him as a puppet leader in a northern Italy. However, in 1945, after the Allies advance, Mussolini and his mistress Claretta Petacci are captured, shot, killed, and hung upside down in the Piazza Loreto in Milan.

1944 — The Allies Storm the Beaches at Normandy

More than 160,000 Allied troops take part in the largest amphibious military landing in history on June 6, 1944, when they storm a 50-mile stretch of the French coastline. The men face heavy artillery fire on beaches that are covered with barbed wire, wooden stakes and other obstacles. More than 9,000 Allied soldiers are killed or wounded, but they pave the way for thousands more to gain a foothold on continental Europe and advance on Nazi troops. The Normandy Invasion, also known as D-Day, leads to the liberation of Paris.

1944 — The G.I. Bill of Rights Becomes Law

Officially known as the Servicemen's Readjustment Act of 1944, the G.I. Bill was created on June 22, 1944 to provide grants for trade school or college tuition, low-interest mortgages and small-business loans, hiring privileges and unemployment payments to veterans. The G.I. Bill makes higher education available to the working class in ways never seen before. Sexist and racist attitudes of the day prevail when the funds are disseminated by the all-white, male staff of the Veterans Administration. Discrimination makes it difficult for female and African-American veterans to actually collect their well-earned benefits.

1944 — Four's the Charm for FDR

President Franklin Delano Roosevelt proves that he's still the crowd-pleasing favorite with American voters when, on November 7, 1944, he is elected to an unprecedented fourth term in office. FDR's ability to lead the country through the Great Depression and the ongoing struggles of World War II contribute to his victory. He defeats the Republican candidate, Governor Thomas Dewey of New York, with a whopping 432 votes in the Electoral College, as compared to Dewey's 99 votes.

1945 — The End of Hitler's War

On May 8, 1945, Allied forces announce the unconditional surrender of Nazi Germany in Europe. Celebrations erupt around the world and the date officially becomes known as Victory in Europe (VE) Day. In London, crowds cheer as King George VI, Queen Elizabeth and Prime Minister Winston Churchill wave from the balcony of Buckingham Palace. In Washington, D.C., President Harry S. Truman dedicates the victory to his predecessor, Franklin Roosevelt, who had died of a cerebral hemorrhage on April 12. Revelers take to the streets all across America, ecstatic that six years of war have finally come to an end. (One week earlier, the Nazi regime crumbled when Adolf Hitler committed suicide in his Berlin bunker, with his new bride, Eva Braun, at his side.)

1945 — Mushroom Clouds Rise in the Far East

As the war in the Pacific continues unabated, President Harry S. Truman gives the order to use the atomic bomb in warfare for the first time. On August 6, 1945, Colonel Paul W. Tibbets, Jr. pilots the Boeing B-29 Superfortress Enola Gay over Hiroshima, Japan, and complies. He drops a bomb code-named "Little Boy" over the city. The destruction is immediate and catastrophic, killing an estimated 80,000 people. Three days later, the United States drops a second atomic bomb on Nagasaki, resulting in another 40,000 casualties.

Above:
Snapshot, labeled "Pilar, 1944."

Below:
Snapshot, praying woman, 1940s.

1945 — V-J Day: Victory Over Japan

On August 14, 1945, Emperor Hirohito announces on national radio that the Japanese forces have surrendered. *The war is over!* Jubilant celebrations break out all across America (and around the world), complete with hordes of shouting, singing, drinking, dancing revelers. Then, on September 2, the formal Japanese Instrument of Surrender is accepted in a ceremony aboard the USS Missouri in Tokyo Bay. U.S. General Douglas MacArthur signs the document on behalf the Allied powers.

```
According to the National World War II
Museum: United States civilian and military
deaths during World War II = 418,500
```

1945 — Joan Crawford: Success and the Single Businesswoman

In September 1945, Warner Brothers releases "Mildred Pierce," the film adaptation of James M. Cain's noir novel. Joan Crawford stars in the title role as a woman who, deserted by her philandering husband, builds her own restaurant empire out of homemade pies, fried chicken and unbridled ambition. With financial success comes a heaping helping of trouble, conflict with her ungrateful daughter — and a cold-blooded murder. Crawford plays the role so well that "Mildred Pierce" earns her the Oscar for Best Actress the following year.

1945 — Pippi Longstocking: A New Freckled Face in Literature

On November 1, the English translation of "Pippi Longstocking" is issued, bringing the adventures of author Astrid Lindgren's plucky, red-haired heroine to the masses. With her suitcase of gold coins and her distinctive pigtails, the fictional (and independently wealthy) Pippi wows a generation of young readers. Nine-year-old Pippi is a dedicated animal lover who lives with her monkey and her horse. Mother is dead; Father is an absentee sea captain. Pippi ignores social conventions and decides to skip school in favor of having adventures. She also possesses superhuman strength and is able to lift her horse with one hand.

1946 — The U.N. Steps Up for the World's Female Population

Established in June of 1946, the United Nation's Commission on the Status of Women (CSW) becomes a global force dedicated to the promotion of gender equality and female empowerment. This intergovernmental policy-making body reaffirms that "all human beings are born free and equal in dignity and rights." The CSW begins to document women's lives all over the globe and sets new standards for gender equality.

Above:
Snapshot, woman on stairs, 1940s.

Opposite Page:
Studio portrait, dated 5-29-45.

Below:
Snapshot, lady shoveling snow, 1946.

Wedding Bells (right):
After the war ends, sweethearts who had postponed marriage during the years of conflict were quick to wed, sometimes in no-frills settings.

According to the National Center for Health Statistics, in 1946, the U.S. marriage rate hit a record high with 16.2 marriages per 1,000 people. However, that same year, the U.S. also experiences an unusual spike in the divorce rate. Some couples who had married in haste before the war found that they weren't really compatible after all. For others, the war had strained their marriages beyond repair and there was simply no going back.

Baby Boom (below):
The war's end also brought about an increase in the U.S. birth rate, with 3.4 million babies being born in 1946 alone! Newlywed couples sought independence from their parents as well as an escape from urban crowding. The suburbs and the dream of homeownership proved irresistable for families just starting out.

1946 — Dirty Diapers? No Longer a Problem!

Tired of dealing with her infant daughter's soggy cloth diapers and the mess they made in her bed, American housewife Marion O'Brien Donovan stitches up a water-tight solution. She takes a cloth diaper, sews a cover of shower curtain plastic over it and calls it "The Boater." Donovan's creation keeps the sheets dry and even reduces her daughter's diaper rash! Eager to build on her idea, Donovan goes one step further and adds plastic snaps, so that safety pins are no longer needed. She receives a patent for her invention, which becomes the first incarnation of the disposable diaper.

1946 — UNICEF Cares for the Little Ones

After World War II, many children living in Europe face terrible living conditions, starvation and rampant disease. On December 11, 1946, the United Nations International Children's Emergency Fund is established, with a headquarters in New York City, as a charitable organization that will work to support them. UNICEF begins providing food, clothing and heath care to children living in areas that have been devastated by the war.

1947 — Debut of the "New Look" by Dior

As America settles into peacetime, women are encouraged to relinquish their jobs, quit thinking, and become homemakers again. Now that fabric rationing is a thing of the past, on February 12, Christian Dior presents a more-is-more fashion statement with his first haute couture collection in Paris. Dior's "New Look," is feminine to the max. It is defined by full skirts, wasp waists and soft, rounded shoulders. The elegant designs make it impossible to actually do much of anything — except look fabulous.

1947 — It's Photo Magic: Polaroid and the Portable Darkroom

Polaroid founder Edwin Land first demonstrates the instant camera on February 21, 1947 at a meeting of the Optical Society of America in New York City. The "Land Camera" contains a roll of positive paper with a pod of developing chemicals at the top of each frame. Turning a knob forces the exposed negative and paper through rollers, which spreads the chemicals evenly between the two layers and pushes the print out of the camera. A paper cutter trims the paper and after a minute, the layers can be peeled apart to reveal — miracle of miracles — a black-and-white photo.

1947 — The Blueprint for Modern Suburbia

In March 1947, sales begin on Levittown, a planned community on Long Island, New York. Levittown homes are designed for returning veterans and their new families and offer an alternative to cramped urban apartments. Assembly-line style production allows for houses to be built quickly — sometimes in as little as one day. The standard Levittown house includes a white picket fence, green lawns, modern appliances and a TV in the living room. With an $8,000 list price ($92,000 in 2019 dollars), and the additional G.I. Bill and federal housing subsidies, the down payment for a new house is as low as $400. In the first three hours that the Levittown homes are on the market, more than 1,400 are snapped up by buyers who are ready to nest.

1947 — Flying Saucers Have Landed

Rancher W.W. Brazel discovers unusual metallic debris scattered across his sheep pasture outside of Roswell, New Mexico on July 7, 1947. He alerts the local sheriff, who is equally perplexed by the find. Officials from a nearby Air Force base claim that it is nothing more than a crashed weather balloon. They even release photos of a military officer holding pieces of the debris, which looks a lot like crumpled tinfoil. UFO enthusiasts don't buy the story. They believe the shiny materials found near Roswell are actually the remnants of a flying saucer. Theories about government scientists retrieving alien bodies from the crash site begin to circulate. The deceased aliens are rumored to have abnormally large heads, elongated eye sockets and spindly little arms and legs. These stories give credence to the unproven notion of "little, green men from outer space" visiting Earth on the sly.

1947 — The Government Wants You to Name Names

It doesn't matter where the perceived enemy is coming from — outer space or down the street — paranoia runs rampant in the United States in the late 1940s. In October, the House Committee on Un-American Activities holds nine days of hearings into alleged Communist propaganda and subversion in the Hollywood movie industry. After being convicted on contempt of

Above:
Snapshot, labeled "Dolores & Ruby, Los Angeles, California," 1940s.

Below:
Studio portrait, young woman wearing a casual "day dress," 1940s.

Above:
Snapshot, woman in spring frock and a hat decorated with fake fruit, 1940s.

Below:
Studio portrait, young lady posing in a woman's suit, 1940s.

Congress for refusing to answer questions, "The Hollywood Ten," receive jail sentences and are blacklisted. Ultimately, hundreds of actors and writers are boycotted by the major studios and their careers are destroyed. Bigger names — such as Charlie Chaplin and Orson Welles — either leave the U.S. or go underground to find work.

1947 — "The Modern Woman: The Lost Sex"

In an effort to convince women to return to their natural (translation: biological) roles as wives and mothers, Marynia Farnham and Ferdinand Lundberg publish "The Modern Woman: The Lost Sex." The message could not have been clearer if the text had simply read: THE WAR IS OVER, YOU LADIES GOTTA GO HOME! Using popularized Freudian analysis as the basis for their theories, Farnham and Lundberg encourage females to joyfully embrace domestic pursuits. And, if they refuse? The authors suggest that women will be solely responsible for all of America's post-war neuroses being transmitted to the next generation. No pressure there.

1947 — Who's On the Jury?

While women might have helped win the war, they still aren't considered appropriate candidates for jury service. In 1947, the U.S. Supreme Court hears the case of *Fay v. New York*, and says that women — unlike men — are not obligated to accept a summons for jury duty. This ruling prevents females from having full participation in the judicial system. It also impacts the execution of the Sixth Amendment's guarantee of a defendant's right to a fair trial with an impartial jury. (Some argue that female jurors might be more inclined to accept an insanity defense than their cold-hearted male counterparts.)

1947 — Oklahoma-Born Ballerina Shows Them How It's Done

The daughter of an Osage tribe member, Maria Tallchief, becomes a trailblazer for Native Americans in the world of ballet. (Prior to her arrival, the art form is dominated by Russian and European dancers.) Tallchief's grace and talent earn her roles with the Ballet Russe de Monte Carlo and the Paris Opera Ballet. After marrying choreographer George Balanchine, who creates her signature "Firebird" role, Tallchief becomes the first prima ballerina of the New City Ballet in 1947.

1947 — "The Diary of a Young Girl" is Published

Fleeing the Nazi occupation of Holland, 13-year-old Anne Frank and her family go into hiding in 1942 in Amsterdam. The Franks and another Jewish family cut themselves off from the outside world by holing up in a

"Secret Annex" in an old office building. For the next two years, they live in cramped, miserable confinement. The two families survive with the help of several friends, including a Dutch woman named Miep Gies, who brings them food and supplies. In the Annex, Frank amuses herself by keeping a diary, a work that encapsulates her day-to-day life as she comes of age in unimaginable wartime conditions. She pens her last entry on August 1, 1944. Three days later, the group is betrayed to the Gestapo and arrested. After Frank's death from typhus in the Bergen-Belsen concentration camp in 1945, Gies finds the diary and returns it to Anne's father, Otto Frank, the family's only survivor, who shares it with the rest of the world.

1947 — An Angel Watches Over the Everglades

After five years of research, freelance journalist Marjory Stoneman Douglas publishes "The Everglades: River of Grass," on November 6, 1947. Her book stresses the importance of conservation in South Florida and decries what unchecked development and industry have already ruined in the area. Douglas makes the case that the Everglades are not a massive expanse of worthless swampland, but a fragile ecosystem that deserves protection. Her book is praised for its scholarly and scientific approach and quickly becomes a bestseller.

1948 — Mrs. Leakey Uncovers a Major Clue to Our Past

While on a dig in Tanzania, British paleoanthropologist Mary Douglas Leakey discovers the first skull fossil of *Proconsul africanus*, an extinct critter that is the ancestor of apes and humans. Her find — which is estimated to be more than 18 million years old — is a key discovery involving the evolution of early human beings in Africa. Even though Mary does most of the digging, her husband and collaborator Louis Leakey generally receives the attention and accolades for their discoveries.

1949 — The North American Treaty Organization (NATO) is Born

In an effort to solidify the postwar peace, the United States, Canada, Belgium, Denmark, France, Iceland, Italy, Luxembourg, Netherlands, Norway, Portugal and the United Kingdom join together to form NATO. The treaty they sign on April 4, 1949 declares that an attack against any one nation would be considered a sign of aggression against them all.

1949 — What a Babe!

It wasn't enough for Babe Didrikson Zaharias to win gold medals in the javelin toss and the 80-meter hurdles in addition to a silver medal in the high jump in the 1932 Los Angeles Olympics. She also wins the women's

Above:
Snapshot, Grandma in the woods, 1940s.

Below:
Studio portrait, lady with corsage, 1940s.

Above:
Snapshot, vamp in the shadows, 1940s.

Opposite Page:
Snapshot, clean-up crew, 1940s.

Bottom:
Snapshot, "Barbara, N.Y., 1949."

amateur golf tournament in 1946 and 17 amateur tournaments afterwards. In 1949, Didrikson Zaharias helps found the LPGA to give women more opportunities to compete in professional golf. The journalists of the Associated Press do her a solid when they vote her Outstanding Woman Athlete of the 20th Century that same year.

1949 — Tokyo Rose Is Sent to the Slammer

On October 7, Iva Toguri, the femme fatale of Japanese war broadcasts, is sentenced to ten years in prison. American-born Toguri, had been caring for her aunt in Japan when the Pearl Harbor attack occurred, effectively stranding her in a country she barely knew. While working as a typist at Radio Tokyo, she is recruited to be the voice of "The Zero Hour" a propaganda show designed to demoralize Allied soldiers in the South Pacific. Toguri claims that she is remaining loyal to the United States by making a farce of her broadcasts, which she does under the name of "Orphan Ann." After the war's end, the U.S. Department of Justice decides that Toguri's broadcasts were "innocuous," but upon her return to America, a public uproar ensues. She is charged, tried and convicted of treason. Toguri maintains her innocence while imprisoned in West Virginia and is paroled in 1956. (President Gerald Ford pardons Toguri in 1977 after two witnesses admit they were pressured into testifying against her.)

1949 — You Think You're Better Than Me?

French author Simone de Beauvoir takes aim at female inequality in 1949 when she unleashes her book "The Second Sex." With her angsty analysis of the treatment of women throughout history, de Beauvoir creates a work that many consider a milestone in feminist philosophy. One issue that particularly goads de Beauvoir is her observation that in contemporary society: "Man defines woman, not in herself, but in relation to himself." Yowzah! By drawing renewed attention to long-simmering issues such as reproductive freedom, female sexuality, and equality in both the home and workplace, "The Second Sex" helps launch a new wave of feminism.

Fashion Footnotes from Photos of the 1940s

The 1940s — "The War Years" (World War II: 1939-1945)

For the duration of 1940s, American women were either fighting in the war; figuring out how to scrimp, save and support the war; worrying about people they loved who were affected by the war; or recovering from the devastation of the war.

Fashion trends from the decade include:

- Dominant Fashion Idea #1: Day-to-day, no-frills utilty clothing; uniforms or clothing for war-related jobs.
- Dominant Fashion Idea #2: Patriotic red, white and blue color palette.
- Dominant Fashion Idea #3: Large padded shoulders; fitted waist; hemlines rise to the knee to save fabric.
- Nylon and silk are rationed; women draw faux hosiery "seams" up the backs of their legs to create the illusion of wearing stockings.
- Big, bold prints replace trim and embellishments (materials which are needed for the military effort) in casual "day dresses."
- In an effort to keep American women's morale high, accessories are not rationed. Whimsical, dramatic or silly hats abound. Platform shoes become popular. Costume jewelry becomes exotic and novel.
- Makeup trends include false eyelashes, penciled arched eyebrows, red lipstick and eyeliner on top lid only.
- Hair is long, but is often tied up in a head scarf or snood for work.
- South American and Central American influences appear in fashion in the form of turbans, peasant blouses and Mexican prints.
- Ladies' Style Icons: Betty Grable, Lana Turner, Rita Hayworth, American actresses and pinup girls.
- In 1947, Christian Dior's "New Look" brings back the use of voluminous fabrics in women's clothing (the end of rationing makes that possible), and ushers in an era of everyday elegance and over-the-top femininity in fashion.

Above:
Snapshot, proud woman posing in her work uniform, 1940s.

Opposite Page:
Studio portrait, labeled on back "Lovely Della Mae," 1940s.

Below:
Snapshot, lady in funkified hat, 1940s. (Note matching hat pin and dress clips!)

Chapter 8:
Spotlight on Technology:
An Ode to the Washing Machine

"We are coming down from our pedestal and up from the laundry room."

— Bella Abzug (1920-1998), American lawyer, U.S. Representative, leader of the women's movement

When my alarm went off at 5:30 this morning, I did not embrace gratitude. The knowledge that it was still dark outside and the weather forecast called for balmy temperatures in the low 20s did not fill my heart with joy. To add insult to injury, I could even hear the wind whipping against my bedroom window. I believe it was whispering, *"Ha, ha… Wake up, Princess! It's time to get up and freeze your ass off!"*

This is Chicago in the winter. It is cold, dark and dank, a place that breeds slothfulness as effortlessly as old bread sprouts mold. I hit the snooze button. Then I scrunched deeper into my pillow and tried to re-enter my dream. It had been a particularly vivid one: I was making peanut-butter-and-jelly sandwiches in my kitchen with Paul and Linda McCartney. We were vegetarian best friends!

Everyone knows the mental anguish that comes from being unceremoniously roused from a dead sleep. It doesn't matter if the culprit is an alarm (iPhone, smoke or otherwise), a wailing baby or a snoring partner — they all pack the same kind of punch.

What did eventually drag me out of bed and into the world today was the realization that my life is enhanced by technology. I did not have to light a kerosene lamp, chop wood or draw water from the well before breakfast. Instead, I jumped right into the day with a small bag of Hostess mini muffins and a Diet Pepsi. *(Health, health, health, darling!)*

The same cannot be said for the females who ran households in the early 20th century. Certainly, the arrival of technological miracles like electric lights, indoor plumbing and the telephone changed American lives dramatically. And yet, women remained virtually shackled to the home environment. Housework could easily fill every waking hour and female domesticity was socially mandated and sanctioned.

However, according to a complex study that I have conducted in my own imagination, with research I

Above:
Lee, Russell, photographer. Housewife boiling clothes, Chicot Farms, Arkansas. United States, 1939. Jan. Photograph. https://www.loc.gov/item/2017738744/.

Previous Spread:
Left: Woman using a copper boiler and a washboard to do the laundry. Early 1900s.

Right: Hand-powered wringer with dual tub system and washboard.
Photo by Kathleen Geraghty.

have done for myself and by myself, I have stumbled upon a radical theory: The electric washing machine set American women free.

Until the late 1800s, home washing machines were hand-powered, which meant that a real human being had to stand there and manually agitate each load of wash. Imagine the excitement that ensued when, in 1908, the Hurley Machine Company of Chicago introduced the Thor, the first commercial electric washing machine! The Thor featured a galvanized tub and an electric motor and it arrived at a time when the U.S. market for home appliances was rapidly expanding.

Today, we can divide the female population into pre- and post-Internet generations. If you want to freak out a young girl, just start a story with, "There were no computers back then. We had to go to the library to look that kind of thing up." You will be met with a look of glassy-eyed horror, an expression that says, *"Who were you? The Flintstones?"* The Thor had the same type of seismic impact on the laundry-related lives of our foremothers: There was a "before" and an "after."

What made this development even more glorious was that the electric washing machine rolled into American society like a majestic, plugged-in Trojan horse. It was filled, not with Greek soldiers, but with hot water, soap suds and the sparkling-clean promise of female independence.

On the surface, it was a symbol of modern prosperity. A man might reason: *"Why make the wife beat my dirty britches upon that mossy rock when I could have her run them through a wash cycle? By golly, the neighbors would be impressed! And then, the little woman could devote more attention to preparing my meals ... I must be fed!"*

The keeping-up-with-the-Joneses aspect of electric washing machine ownership had its appeal. That's why men, who generally controlled the household budgets back in the day, would approve and fund such purchases. However, in buying these newfangled washing machines, husbands did something infinitely more valuable: They created free time for their wives. And we all know that nothing is more dangerous than a female who has plenty of time to think about what she really wants.

Just exactly how much drudgery did the electric washing machine eliminate? Thank you for asking! In the 1800s, most women used a large, copper boiler to wash clothes. It was placed on top of the kitchen stove — an appliance that was a heat-belching, wood or coal-burning monstrosity. Water could then be heated and bar soap would be grated and added to the steaming cauldron. Clothes were swished around in the copper boiler

Above:
Left: Woman in full "Gibson Girl" regalia, posing at outdoor water pump, 1900s.

Right: Washboard, linens, laundry basket and clothesline reel, early 1900s.
Photo by Kathleen Geraghty.

Below:
Advertisement for the Thor electric washing machine, 1920.

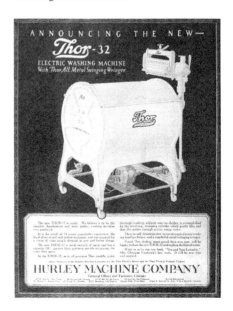

with a big, old stick or a plunger-type device called a "dolly." In rural areas, the same laundry-sanitizing system could be completed over an open fire outdoors. The washboard-and-tub combo was also very common. Unfortunately, that system involved a lot of toting and schlepping of water. The slow and sloshy process meant that it could take as long as two full days to wash, dry and iron the week's laundry.

In the mid-1800s, several types of early washing machines were developed, but all required that the laundry be agitated with a hand-powered cranking mechanism. After washing, the sopping wet clothes were run through a wringer to squeeze out the excess water.

Though the idea of the completely electric washing machine had been bandied about for several years, it wasn't until 1908, when the Thor was first marketed in the United States, that the new technology became a bubbly sensation. In the decades ahead, electricity would usher in even more efficient models of the washing machine. The process of spinning the washing drum at a high speed in a perforated container was eventually developed to allow centrifugal force to dry clothes in a faster, safer manner.

Above:
Snapshot, late 1900s or early 1910s.

Below:
Suffragette Pickets. Date Created/Published: [between 1910 and 1920]. Reproduction Number: LC-DIG-hec-13815. Harris & Ewing Photographs - http://www.loc.gov/rr/print/res/140_harr.html

Opposite Page:
Washing machine advertisement, *The Saturday Evening Post*, February 26, 1921. Ad copy states that a woman should take her husband along in order to shop for a washing machine because, "one feels ever so much better satisfied when one's husband gives his approval in such an important purchase."

The wringer system was then phased out, putting an end to gruesome laundry-related injuries that involved fingers, hands, hair, or articles of clothing getting caught in the mechanism.

When the washing machine went full-on electric, it sparked a change in the lives of American women. Posh ladies no longer needed to employ large staffs of domestic workers to handle the weekly household laundry. Without as many people to supervise, these well-heeled women had greater ability to socialize and volunteer their time in their communities.

In turn, fewer domestic workers were needed to labor in large homes, so young working women sought employment in stores, factories and offices, thereby expanding the female presence in the American workplace. As time went on, these women took part in industrial protests, strikes and reform groups, all of which helped strengthen labor's bargaining power.

Once the household laundry was no longer a two-day marathon of hard labor, women were free to pursue new interests and goals. The electric washing machine truly was the start of something big.

This truth was never more apparent to me than it was this morning, post-Diet Pepsi. In an effort to delay my encounter with Chicago's winter, I took a moment to put a load of towels in the washing machine. As I poured fabric softener into the rotating water-filled drum, I could just make out the tiniest, metallic voice gurgling, *"Free at last, free at last, thank God Almighty we're free at last ... "*

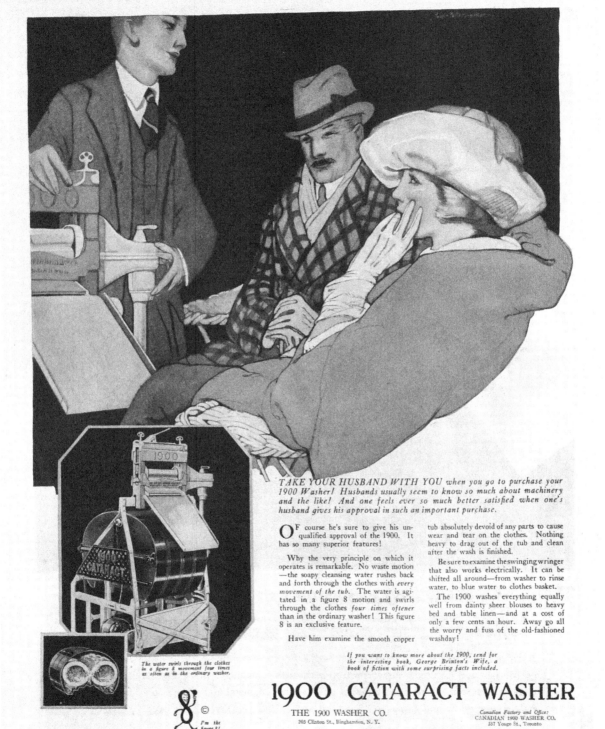

The water swirls through the clothes in a figure 8 movement four times as often as in the ordinary washer.

TAKE YOUR HUSBAND WITH YOU when you go to purchase your 1900 Washer! Husbands usually seem to know so much about machinery and the like! And one feels ever so much better satisfied when one's husband gives his approval in such an important purchase.

OF course he's sure to give his unqualified approval of the 1900. It has so many superior features!

Why the very principle on which it operates is remarkable. No waste motion—the soapy cleansing water rushes back and forth through the clothes with *every movement of the tub*. The water is agitated in a figure 8 motion and swirls through the clothes *four times oftener* than in the ordinary washer! This figure 8 is an exclusive feature.

Have him examine the smooth copper tub absolutely devoid of any parts to cause wear and tear on the clothes. Nothing heavy to drag out of the tub and clean after the wash is finished.

Be sure to examine the swinging wringer that also works electrically. It can be shifted all around—from washer to rinse water, to blue water to clothes basket.

The 1900 washes everything equally well from dainty sheer blouses to heavy bed and table linen—and at a cost of only a few cents an hour. Away go all the worry and fuss of the old-fashioned washday!

If you want to know more about the 1900, send for the interesting book, George Brinton's Wife, a book of fiction with some surprising facts included.

1900 CATARACT WASHER

I'm the figure 8!

THE 1900 WASHER CO.
203 Clinton St., Binghamton, N. Y.

Canadian Factory and Office:
CANADIAN 1900 WASHER CO.
357 Yonge St., Toronto

Chapter 9:
C'mon Over, It's Party Time!

"Of course I know how to roll a joint."

— *Martha Stewart (1941-), American entrepreneur, lifestyle guru, TV personality and convicted felon*

You know what I love? Chit-chat, food and frivolity. The beauty of gathering with others is that sometimes when I am experiencing a low ebb or a karmic freakout, bitching my head off with others is a great way to clear out the cobwebs.

Maybe you feel the same. Let me ask: Do you hate your job? Your spouse? Your life? Are you sick and tired of being sick and tired? A "Thanks to Her" party might be just the kick in the tuchas you need to get to higher ground. If you live in a state that has legalized marijuana in recent months — as Illinois has — there are many additional ways to reach higher ground. You are welcome to employ those as well. It's a free country!

As a matter of fact, if someone does bring a hostess gift of pot brownies to your "Thanks to Her" soiree, it can be a conversation starter. Compare and contrast: the repeal of Prohibition in the 1930s and the de-criminalization of cannabis in the 2020s. Talk amongst yourselves!

That said, a "Thanks to Her" photo-fest can take any number of forms. You can spend a solo evening at home in flannel PJs, digging around in your family archive and dancing to Martha and the Vandellas. Or, you can invite a few friends over for casual cocktails and chick flicks and make the photo retrospective an entertainment sidebar. If you're an overachiever, you can go big and bougie, with multimedia components and exotic dancers in a rented ballroom! The point is, it's your party, they're your photos, and you can cry if you want to. *(You said it, Lesley Gore!)*

There's only one suggestion I would like to offer: Ask your guests to bring a few of their own family photographs along to share and discuss. Otherwise, the whole event takes on a narcissistic "come-to-my-house-and-let's-talk-about-me" tone. That vibe recalls the dreaded "Grand Canyon Vacation Slideshow" torture that was inflicted upon many a captive dinner party guest in the 1950s.

Personally, I think a "Thanks to Her" party can be a new frontier — kind of like a Wild, Wild West of photo-fueled group therapy. It's an opportunity for all guests to leave their troubles out on the front porch, their emotional baggage in the foyer and their casseroles in the kitchen. It's a chance to let down our hair (real or faux), swap stories and celebrate our collective female history. Let's pay homage to all those women who sacrificed and stepped up over and over and over again so that future generations might benefit.

Who Should Participate in This Love Fest?

The guest list for a "Thanks to Her" celebration is completely flexible. Invite anyone whose company you enjoy and who is not currently on house arrest. A few helpful hints:

- People who are accomplished cooks or professional chefs are a party plus; they will cheerfully supply creative and tasty hors d'oeuvres. This takes one chore off your hostess "to-do" checklist and allows more time for perfuming yourself before the main event.
- Highly educated guests are handy for conducting online research during the gathering. These individuals can tackle historical questions such as: Who was the first female OB-GYN in America? Did Billie Holiday have a dog? When was hairspray invented?
- Chronically happy women are an asset, as they can balance the group's energy if anyone in the room is suffering from horrible cramps or the mood-dampening effects of a bad haircut.
- Guests who are 70-plus years old are incredible party attendees because they no longer feel the need to self-censor or sugarcoat the truth. They also remember what the 1960s were *really* all about.
- Women who have young children at home will be thrilled to attend and will arrive early. They are so grateful for adult conversation and the opportunity to use their "big girl" vocabularies that they will happily stay late to help tidy up your kitchen.
- Guests who are less than 25 years old have tremendous energy and are a boon to any "Thanks to Her" gathering, large or small. They can document the event by taking selfies and videos. They will also execute a full-blown social media marketing plan before the rest of the crowd is done sampling the jalapeño cheese ball.
- A guest who is struggling with serious illness or grieving the loss of a loved one should be given the comfiest chair in the house, a feather boa and a tiara. Everyone in attendance is required to bring her refreshments on command and curtsy while serving them. This individual is given priority access to the powder room and is allowed to cut in line, no questions asked. During the event, she should be addressed as "Your Majesty."
- Consider adding a few heavy drinkers to the mix. They are jovial folk, prone to sleeping overnight on your couch and drooling on your

Above:
Vintage party invitation, 1930s.
Photograph by Kathleen Geraghty.

Previous Spread:
Left: Snapshot, woman posing by formal dining room table. Captioned on the back: "Burling Street Surprise Party," late 1930s or early 1940. This appears to be a table that is set for dinner for 15 people. Can you imagine the incredible amount of work that went into hosting this event, in an era when the American kitchen did not include a dishwasher, food processor or microwave?

Right: Two elegant ladies in a mid-century living room. Back of snapshot inscribed "Weazie & Florence, 1950."

throw pillows. Who else can you count on to lift up her shirt to show off her new brassiere? Your favorite barfly, that's who!
- Remember: Life is short and this is meant to be a safe space. If the moon and stars align and all things are as they should be, a "Thanks to Her" gathering will become a magical convergence of sisterhood, inspiration and hilarity.

Do I Dare Attempt a Theme?

To me, a theme party is a little bit of Halloween plopped right down in the middle of everyday living. Of course, it does require some effort.

If you are a theatrical gal at heart, encourage your guests to dress in early 20th century garb or wear something that was handed down to them — a hat, a corset, a pin — the sky's the limit. Participation is purely voluntary. Not everyone enjoys the challenge of pulling together a unique outfit. Those who are in a low-energy state of mind can be invited to just space out and bask in the all-girl atmosphere.

Serving refreshments that reflect a certain era can be super-fun. It is for this reason that I have concocted a simple plan for a Great Depression-themed "Thanks to Her" party. I should clarify that while I was doing the research for this book, I fell in love with the 1930s in a way I never expected. It was a decade of widespread economic trouble and need, that is certain. But, it was also a time in which American women took control of what little they had, got inventive, and whipped up a million tiny miracles.

1930s Theme Tip #1: The Visuals Set the Mood

- Tablecloth: Go with burlap, old fabric or sheets of newspaper.
- Napkins: Cut old towels or rags into 12-inch squares and use rubber bands or bread bag twist-ties as napkin rings.
- Drinking Glasses: Opt for jelly jars or tin cans or anything else that discreetly inquires, *"Sister, can you spare a dime?"*
- Silverware: Choose mismatched, metal and beat up. (Plastic utensils debuted in the 1940s and were not mass produced until the 1950s.)
- Centerpiece: Fill a coffee can with dandelions or swamp weeds.
- Coffee Table: Offer nibbles that were introduced in the 1930s: Snickers, Kit Kat and 3 Musketeers candy bars; Lay's Potato Chips and Fritos Corn Chips; Tootsie Pops and Cinnamon Red Hots.

The idea here is to use what you already have on hand. Purchasing the food and drink should be your only expense, and if you really want to get serious, the menu should be representative of the time period. If you feel that you absolutely must buy something, get a hostess outfit from a thrift store. Do not wash it, wear it wrinkly and leave the price tag on. Another

KITCHENETTE COOKERY

The Secret Ingredient? It's Not Apples!
When Ritz Crackers debuted in 1934, their buttery flavor and glamorous name made them a hit with thrifty homemakers. By 1935, Nabisco had introduced a recipe for "Ritz Cracker Mock Apple Pie" to capitalize on its success. The filling required only crumbled Ritz Crackers and no real fruit.

kicky wardrobe option is a stained t-shirt with holes in it, accented with your favorite costume jewelry. Perhaps this is already your standard attire. In that case, you will not have to search far and wide for your party ensemble and are ready to roll.

1930s Theme Tip #2: Music Makes Your Party a Hit

Some of the most popular tunes of the Great Depression era were designed to make people think that economic recovery was right around the corner and everything was gonna be *just fine*. For example, actress Ethel Merman introduced the hit song "Life is Just a Bowl of Cherries" while performing on Broadway in "George White's Scandals," a 1931 stage revue.

That catchy little ditty suggested that existence was nothing but a wacky riddle tied up in a sugar-coated mystery. Why, there was no need scramble around in frantic pursuit of the elusive dollar! Everyone should just revel in the folly of it all, and laugh, laugh, laugh!

Additional keep-your-chin-up tunes from the 1930s included:
- "I Got Rhythm," George and Ira Gershwin, 1930
- "Hello, I Must Be Going," Groucho Marx in "Animal Crackers," 1930
- "It Don't Mean A Thing (If It Ain't Got That Swing)," Duke Ellington and His Famous Orchestra with Ivie Anderson vocals, 1932
- "We're In The Money," Ginger Rogers in "Gold Diggers of 1933"
- "On The Good Ship Lollipop," Shirley Temple in "Bright Eyes," 1934
- "You're The Top," Cole Porter, 1934
- "What A Little Moonlight Can Do," Billie Holiday, 1935
- "Bei Mir Bist Du Schön," The Andrews Sisters, 1937
- "A Tisket, A Tasket," Ella Fitzgerald, 1938
- "Back in the Saddle Again," Gene Autry, 1939

If you're old-school about music and doing research, libraries are a fine resource for 1930s compilation CDs. Digital divas can turn to YouTube for playlists that will have your guests singin' and swingin' in no time flat!

1930s Theme Tip #3: The No-Frills Menu

During the 1930s, when the Great Depression put roughly 25 percent of the country on the unemployment line, women, in turn, got very creative when it came to putting food on the kitchen table.

In rural areas, this meant gophers, rabbits, squirrels, turtles — and even roadkill — could be used to cook up a pot of stew. Cows and goats provided milk, which was a godsend. Families who were lucky enough to have chickens wasted nothing. They fried up the skin for sandwiches and used the feet to flavor broth. Of course, chickens were a source of eggs

Above:
Studio portraits, 1930s.

which could be cooked in a myriad of ways, so people could not afford to be hasty in chopping off any heads. City dwellers, unfortunately, had fewer options when it came to hunting game or raising livestock.

Many American families learned to love no-fuss entrees like Pork and Beans, Macaroni and Cheese, and Chipped Beef on Toast. Easily grown vegetables such as potatoes, onions, peppers, spinach, cabbage, tomatoes and carrots were mainstays, while the three Bs — bologna, bacon and beans — were inexpensive sources of protein. Lunchtime sandwiches were often made with scrambled eggs, peanut butter, ketchup, or even bacon grease, and dressed up with lettuce, onions and pickles.

1930s Theme Tip #4: Manners Are the Key to Success

Since my parents could not afford to send me to Sears Charm School back in the day, I offer you these vintage words of party-planning wisdom from "The New Book of Etiquette," the updated edition of which was written by Lillian Eichler in 1939:

> "To be a successful hostess does not necessarily mean that one must have a twenty-one room house and a staff of servants. Of course, one does not give a highly ceremonious dinner, or a formal, elaborate luncheon, in a house that is not well-organized and well-appointed — or if one does not have the skill, the service, the furnishings, the tact essential to such functions. Nor does a novice who has had but little experience attempt a formal dinner with all its important details.
>
> But it is possible to be a successful hostess even in the most humble home with the most modest furnishings; for, after all, hospitality is of the heart rather than the pocketbook. Graceful and kindly hospitality does not depend upon material things. It is the personality of the hostess, not her linens and silver, that makes her popular and makes people enjoy being invited to her home.
>
> The successful hostess is not she who can display the richest silver, but she who knows how to make her guests feel comfortable and happy. Not she who can serve the most elaborate and unusual courses, but she who can hold the most interesting conversations and draw people into the most pleasant discussions ... In a truer sense, hospitality does not attempt to give what it does not have — it shares what it has."

PARTY SUGGESTIONS

There's Always Room for Jell-O!
When a hostess wanted a touch of elegance for her dinner table, she could present a Jell-O mold with an exotic name. Among the recipes promoted by Jell-O in the 1930s were: Roman Sponge; Oriental Compote; Charlotte Russe Imperial; Jelly Sahara; and Hawaiian Sunset Mold.

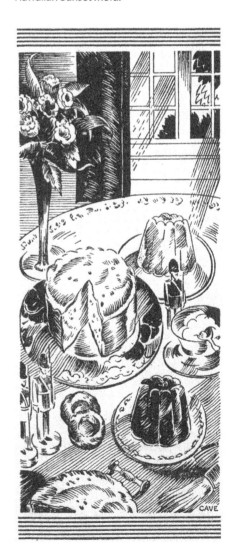

Mix It All Together and You'll Make Magic!

A Chicken in Every Pot? Not Exactly ...

During the Great Depression, the one-pot meal became a go-to staple of American cuisine. At the neediest end of the economic food spectrum were the hobos, unemployed men who would hop freight trains to travel across the country in search of work. For hobos, finding food was a constant struggle. However, by begging scraps of meat and vegetables from butchers, grocers, farm wives or other charitable individuals, a hobo could whip up a pretty decent "Mulligan Stew." The proper cooking technique involved a tin can and an open campfire.

In a similar vein, when armed with a casserole dish and ingenuity, the average American woman could stretch her pennies as far as humanly possible. The truth was that just about anything edible could be chopped, smashed and mixed with bread crumbs and egg. The resulting food ball could then be artistically molded into a lump and baked until it was a 3D culinary sculpture, ready for slicing.

Women's magazines and daily newspapers provided inspiration in the form of hundreds of scary "loaf" recipes. These championed the use of beans, liver and nuts as affordable sources of dietary protein and suitable replacements for actual meat. Needless to say, this kind of bait-and-switch did not fool anyone who was dreaming of a T-bone steak or lamb chops. Here's a sample recipe from the *Chicago Daily Tribune*:

Above:
Snapshot, Depression Era woman hangin' out with the chickens in the yard, 1930s.

Pea Roast (1930s Style)

- 1 egg, well beaten
- 1 tablespoon of sugar
- ¼ cup melted butter
- ½ cup pea pulp (canned or dried)
- ¼ cup finely chopped peanuts
- ¾ cup whole milk
- ¾ cup stale bread crumbs
- Salt and pepper to taste

Blend the melted butter with sugar and eggs. Mix together the pea pulp, peanuts, seasonings, bread crumbs, and milk and combine with the first mixture. Turn into a greased pan and bake in oven at 350 degrees for 25 minutes. Serve with tomato sauce or chopped pickle. Serves four.*

* If You Want To Know More
This recipe was reprinted in a wonderful book that I invite you to check out if you are interested in learning about American food in the 1930s. It covers the subject in great detail and provides background on the resurgence of regional cooking, the formation of the U.S. government's nutrition guidelines, the evolution of home economics and test kitchens, and the growth of the frozen food industry. It also examines hobo culture, which is valuable information, if you ask me.

"A Square Meal: A Culinary History of the Great Depression," by Jane Ziegelman and Andrew Coe. New York, Harper Collins Publishers, 2016.

You Can Always Smother It in Sauce!

Another invaluable tool for the 1930s chef was White Sauce. It was the touch of elegance that could be added to all sorts of lackluster entrées and side dishes. While the standard White Sauce was made of flour, butter and milk, it could be jazzed up with additional ingredients like parsley, mustard, onion, celery, peppers or cheese. White Sauce gave economical recipes like "Codfish Surprise" and "Spaghetti-Corn Cakes" their bland charm. It was also used to thicken soups, glue croquettes together and cover a multitude of sins in the name of all things "scalloped."

In researching what a Great Depression-themed party might look like, I reviewed a number of vintage cookbooks and magazine articles. The *Chicago Daily News* editors, in their 1930 cookbook, recommended that the average housewife should establish a family food budget of $4 per person per week if she wanted to make ends meet. In 2020 dollars, that would be approximately $60 per person, per week. I suppose that's fair. But, when there's no work, $4 might as well be $4 million and Dandelion Soup for dinner sounds like it would be just perfect.

Above:
Nothing says "Happy Days Are Here Again" like serving beverages in authentic 1930s New Deal mugs. Not only are they shaped like beer barrels, they feature the profile of President Franklin Delano Roosevelt!

In 1933, FDR signed the Beer and Wine Revenue Act, which amended the Volstead Act of 1919 and legalized the sale of beer and wine that contained no more than 3.2 percent alcohol. The act levied a federal tax on all alcoholic beverages (thus raising much-needed money for the U.S. government) and gave each state the option to regulate the future sale and distribution of beer and wine.

I like to pair my own New Deal mugs with raggedy, mismatched napkins. They really come in handy when we're cooking up franks and beans on the outdoor fireplace. Photograph by Kathleen Geraghty.

Family Parties: Expect the Unexpected!

It's possible that you might have to do a bit of cajoling to get your daughter, sister, mother and other female relations to join you in a "Thanks to Her" photo-editing session. This is not a situation in which the "go-big-or-go-home" mentality will be conducive to success. Do not expect miracles or weeping or laughing or even enthusiastic participation right off the bat. Envision yourself sitting alone at the dining room table, quietly flipping through pictures while everyone else gathers in the front room, basking in the hypnotic glow of our old friend TV.

> The key to hosting a "Thanks to Her" party for your extended family members is to set your expectations very low.

Then, when things actually turn out well, you can celebrate! When your cousins stop bickering for five minutes to study the vintage portrait of your grandmother in her wedding dress, you can consider it a win. And if your grandmother is able to refrain from smoking her cigar long enough to study the photo and share her recollections of the day ... you're golden!

Provide the food, beverages and tableware that will inspire the type of photo-editing party you desire. China and silver are perfect if you're going all Jackie-Kennedy-debutante-chic. Pork rinds with hot sauce and Budweisers on ice can set the stage for a low-rent festival of fun that people will talk about for years! It's your family history — you're the art director and you can shine the spotlights on whatever you choose.

Another key to this process is to ask open-ended questions, which are broad and can be answered in detail. (As opposed to close-ended questions, which require a yes, no, or simple factual response.) Be sure to avoid hot-button queries such as, *"Why were you so fat in this picture?"*

During the event, the creation of audio recordings, video recordings and selfies should be encouraged. Aside from documenting the get-together, they can be useful in the future in a court of law, if your party takes a dark turn and goes completely off the rails.

Above:
Mystery woman and baby, photobooth portrait, late 1930s.

Why was the lady hiding from the camera? Was she having a bad hair day? Was the baby actually hers? Did the baby have a loaded diaper? We will never know.

Opposite Page:
Mystery woman and sedan, 1929.

OK, so I have a *million* questions about the photo on the opposite page. Who was this woman? Was she a recent immigrant? Did she travel in the car parked behind her? Why is the door open? Was she carsick? Did she need fresh air? Is somebody going to drop her off like a murder weapon on that park bench and drive away?

Black Thursday and the stock market crash took place a few months after this photo was taken. What happened to this lady during the Great Depression?

This is why it's important to ask these questions now, while the people who can answer them are still alive and well. I don't know about you, but these kinds of things keep me awake at night ...

Chapter 10: Considering the "Big Picture"

"Every great dream begins with a dreamer. Always remember, you have within you the strength, the patience, and the passion to reach for the stars to change the world."

— *Harriet Tubman (1822-1913), American abolitionist, conductor in the Underground Railroad*

Here's a question to ponder: How do you value yourself when you exist in a society that does not value you? For early 20th century American women, the solution to this quandary was multifaceted. Of course, given the societal pressures of the time, it meant that a little subterfuge was necessary.

In 1900, women did not have the right to vote in public elections. So, while they lived in a robust democracy, they were not participatory citizens. Once married, a woman gave up her last name, becoming instead a new hybrid persona — Mrs. John Smith or some such. Women were believed to be a "weaker sex," lagging behind men not only in physical strength, but in intelligence and emotional maturity.

Circa 1900, females were valued for being pious, pure and modest in behavior. Middle and upper-class ladies were submissive and dependent on their fathers or husbands for protection and financial security. If all of this pigeonholing wasn't stifling enough, it was widely accepted that a woman's place was in the home, not in business or politics. In other words, she might have had a brain, but she was not encouraged to turn it on. What might this saintly creature do once she got tired of fluttering around in her gilded cage? For amusement, women of financial means could spend countless hours shopping at one of the new, opulent department stores, such as Macy's or Bloomingdale's in New York City, Marshall Field's or Carson Pirie Scott in Chicago, and Wanamaker's in Philadelphia. These emporiums tapped into female boredom and provided a safe, welcoming environment where they could browse without chaperones or male companions — and spend money to their heart's content. (If a lady preferred to lounge about at home, she could flip through the Sears, Roebuck & Company mail order catalog and buy anything from clothing and jewelry to appliances and hardware.)

This type of leisure was unfathomable to poor women, who had to work in dangerous factories, mills, and laundries or in back-breaking agricultural jobs in

Previous Spread:
Left: Studio portrait, 1900s.
Right: Du Bois, W. E. B., collector; Askew, T. E., photographer. (1899) Nine African American women, full-length portrait, seated on steps of a building at Atlanta University, Georgia. Library of Congress, https://www.loc.gov/item/95507098/.

order to survive. And those department stores that were so swell? If a female of lesser means was really lucky, she might find employment as a shop girl. She could stand on her feet all day to sell the finery, but she certainly couldn't afford to purchase any of it.

Immigrant women, hampered by language and cultural barriers, faced their own unique challenges. In urban tenements, working at home to earn money became popular when the piecework system, originated by German tailors, made it possible for parts of garments to be sewn at home, then delivered to the factory. Immigrant mothers and their children often labored side-by-side on projects as diverse as fine embroidery, knitting, stringing beads, making artificial flowers, shelling nuts or rolling cigarettes.

Farm wives had a much different lifestyle, one that involved work both inside the house and outdoors. (Those cows weren't going to milk themselves!) The only benefit of having to engage in physical labor — aside from the cardio — was that it made wearing a corset virtually impossible. So, while they might have been strapped for cash, many rural women were not necessarily strapped into the waist-nipping costumes of the day.

African-American women carried the dual burdens of sexism and racism. Many were employed as maids, nannies, dressmakers, laundresses, waitresses and farm laborers. They did so in a nation that sanctioned a doctrine of "separate but equal," the result of the 1896 U.S. Supreme Court ruling in *Plessy v. Ferguson*. Racial segregation was the law of the land and in the South it went by the name of Jim Crow.

And yet, regardless of their social status, all American women were charged with running the family home and raising the children at a time when their opinions were of little value. How incongruous it was that the ladies, the second-class citizens, were given the most important job of all: nurturing the next generation and ensuring the very future of our country.

The Power of the Caregiver

Motherhood in the early 20th century was fraught with peril and worry. Illness could strike at any moment and often it did, with catastrophic results. According to the Center for Disease Control, in 1900 in some American cities, up to 30 percent of infants died before reaching their first birthday. So, what did women do? They stepped up and made child care into an art form. Motherhood became more than a biological imperative: It became a calling, one that required creativity, dedication and the will to succeed, against all odds.

With the dark threat of infectious disease constantly hovering over their lives, American women turned to medical science for solutions. By adopting new methods of care and forging partnerships with local doctors, mothers were able to dramatically improve their children's well-being. However, this had to be accomplished in racially segregated fashion.

White male physician leadership had created a separate health subsystem for African-Americans and the poor. Many hospitals, clinics, and doctor's offices were racially segregated.

While the nation's physicians might have pitched the ideas, it was the ladies who championed the germ theory of disease, the surgical treatment of illness and the pasteurization of the milk supply. (Think about that the next time your mother tells you to wash your hands!)

Better still, American women had combined the social goals of motherhood and the emerging science of pediatrics to launch a new child-protection movement. This effort grew in tandem with the rise in Progressive-Era journalism and the struggle to improve living conditions in overcrowded city slums. Middle-class women were particularly vocal ambassadors who endorsed reform as a means of caring for poor, orphaned or sick children.

As conventional wisdom called for a movement away from child labor to better healthcare and education for youngsters, American women led the charge. Reformers such as Lillian Wald, (who founded the Henry Street Settlement in New York City), Jane Addams (who founded Hull House in Chicago), and social worker Grace Abbott spoke up and advocated for the nation's children. Their efforts inspired President Theodore Roosevelt to call the first White House Conference on the Care of Dependent Children in 1909. In addressing the conference, Roosevelt likened the role of a mother who raises healthy, well-bred children to that of the "solider who fights for his country."

The middle-class ideal of the sacred family with the father as the breadwinner was not feasible for all Americans. Furthermore, the poor did not have the luxury of shielding their children from the harsh realities of life. What kept these families afloat was a network of altruistic caregivers.

For many generations, farm wives had shared resources with their neighbors. They gave what they had and asked for what they needed. This system of mutual assistance worked beautifully for everyone. In the same spirit, women who banded together to provide child care at settlement houses, community nurseries, and in their own homes, helped create a paradigm shift. They embraced the very basic and intuitive "it takes a village" approach to nurturing the young — and it worked. By the 1910s, it was commonly accepted that the economic and social progress of the nation was based upon the physical, mental and moral health of its children.

The Next Hurdle

After kicking ass on the child-rearing issue, American women decided to shake things up a bit. Their inability to participate in the democratic process had become increasingly annoying. During World War I, men left their jobs on farms, in factories and in offices to become soldiers. Women, always

Above:
Studio portrait, late 1910s.

Opposite Page:
Top: Studio portrait, 1910s.
Bottom: Studio portrait, 1900s.

Below:
Snapshot, 1910s.

ready to pick up the slack, took their places. They harvested crops, balanced the books, answered phones and kept businesses afloat. Some brave females ventured overseas to serve as nurses, translators and ambulance drivers.

After the Great War ended and the Treaty of Versailles was signed in 1919, many American women demurely returned to hearth and home. The ones who remained in the U.S. labor force were relegated to "feminine" jobs such as maids, cooks, secretaries and nurses. Coincidentally, these positions did not pay as well as jobs traditionally held by men. *Say what?*

It came to pass that society ladies, working girls, women of color, immigrant women and downtrodden females living in poverty all started comparing notes. Socially, they were worlds apart, but when it came to getting duped, these gals were all on the same page. Women's rights organizations began to fire up their long-simmering battle against gender oppression. They fought for equal opportunities for women in employment, higher education and all aspects of American society.

Years of public protesting and hunger-striking finally brought about the desired result when, in 1920, the U.S. Congress ratified the 19th Amendment, giving American women the right to vote. While every dowager, dame and diva could now have a ballot all her own, the amendment did not completely level the playing field. It failed to guarantee equal pay and did not require employers to provide equal professional opportunities to female workers. It also had no impact on racial discrimination.

Getting Credentials

Looking for yet another way to enrich themselves and exercise their chutzpah, American women turned to education. They hit the books in eras when their intellectual development was considered a stone-cold waste of time. While higher education was affordable to just a small percentage of Americans, the number of female high school and college graduates steadily increased during the early 20th century. (According to the National Center for Education Statistics, in 1900, there were 85,000 females enrolled in U.S. institutions of higher learning in the United States. By 1950, the number of female students in colleges and universities was 721,000.)

Due to this cultural shift, the nation benefited from a proliferation of newly-accredited female teachers, nurses and social workers. Armed with academic credentials, women also began to make slow *(very slow)* inroads into traditionally male areas such as business, science, medicine, journalism, law and engineering.

Despite having the right to vote and the desire to participate in endeavors outside of the home, American women found that true equality was still out of reach. Ever resourceful, they seized opportunities for growth wherever they could. Females might have been denied roles of political and economic power, but they continued to organize, lobby and protest at the

This Spread:

Above: Graduation portrait of Octavia C. Long, June 1909. Collection of the Smithsonian National Museum of African American History and Culture.
Opposite Page: Graduation portrait, 1910s.
Below: Graduation portrait, 1920s.

Above:
Studio portrait, inscribed on back "Aunt Goldie," 1920s.

Below:
Honor roll of women who will work to win the war: Has he registered your name for service? / The Edgell Company, Phila. United States, 1917. [Philadelphia: Civilian Service and Labor Dept] Library of Congress, https://www.loc.gov/item/00652935/.

grassroots level. They fought for better wages and working conditions, held leadership positions on local school boards and ran community outreach programs through churches, synagogues and other religious organizations.

This kind of work paid off in the long run, as it helped to fuel bigger social changes. For example, by the 1920s, the National Association for the Advancement of Colored People had evolved from a biracial coalition of progressives into a sophisticated organization that led the fight against racial violence, discrimination in employment, segregated public facilities and denial of voting rights. Its members were still organizing locally, as they had since the NAACP's founding in 1909, but they were now lobbying for change at the federal levels of government.

War: What Is It Good For? You Tell Me.

Modern technology offered the ladies new freedoms, with the automobile being one contraption that particularly broadened their horizons. Motor vehicles gave an already mobile people the means to travel further, faster and more spontaneously. The nation's desire to hit the road was palpable and the U.S. auto industry was happy to assist. (In 1929, more than 5.3 million new cars rolled off the assembly line, a record that would not be surpassed or even matched for 20 years.)

As industrialization led to the rapid growth of urban areas, women transitioned from farm labor and domestic service to employment as clerks and factory workers. However, nothing shakes up the status quo like a war, and during the first half of the 20th century, American women lived through TWO of them. While bullets were flying overseas, the traditional social order back in the United States was downright discombobulated. These shifts brought about new opportunities for employment and on-the-job training for females.

Perhaps an even more powerful tangential effect of military conflict was the transmission of new ideas to women. U.S. war propaganda during both World War I and World War II told them they were essential to victory. *(Hey, if Uncle Sam wants me, I must have some kind of value, right?)* This type of radical messaging — sanctioned by the all-knowing American government — convinced the ladies that they were productive and capable citizens. Patriotism did the rest.

There was no question that females took matters into their own dishpan hands and entered the workforce in times of trouble. They willingly made sacrifices in order to support their families and their beloved country when the chips were down. Unfortunately, they were not absolved from their child-rearing duties. Who minded the precious children while Mother was on the job, toting her weary load? Why, it was the handy caregiving network of grandmothers, aunties, sisters and apple-pie-baking neighbors, of course! Remember those folks?

Women Drivers:

In the early 20th century, the idea of "women drivers" (a pejorative term that exists to this day) heading out on the open road threatened the status quo. This was an era in which females were not encouraged to leave their communities — or their front porches, for that matter — without a male chaperone. The automobile not only broadened their horizons, it introduced them to ideas and situations that were outside of the domestic realm.

When women took the wheel, they set out to explore; they traveled distances far greater than the family horse and buggy had permitted. The very sight of a woman driver was disruptive in that automobile ownership suggested social and economic power — two things that American women did not possess in the Victorian and Edwardian eras.

By the 1910s, the automobile had moved beyond being a "passing fad" or a toy for the wealthy. The emergence of female drivers coincided with the increasing debate over women's rights and their ability to step into public life via the ballot box and the university. The ladies were getting defiant!

The combination of automobile mass production (which reduced the price of new cars), the social upheaval of World War I, and the suffrage movement all worked together to offer women new opportunities.

There were less than 7 million passenger cars registered in the United States in 1919. Just a decade later, at the end of the Roaring Twenties, more than 23 million cars were registered. Women were driving automobiles, voting, bobbing their hair, drinking gin, dancing The Charleston, showing their legs, and smoking cigarettes in public. Talk about a metamorphosis!

Above:
Snapshot, Location unknown, but thought to be United States, West Coast, 1930s.

When married American women competed for lucrative employment opportunities, they also faced the stigma of being considered "selfish." It was thought that if a gal had a husband, she should bow out and relinquish a job to an unemployed man that might be loafing around nearby, looking all useless and pitiful. After all, that would have been the "ladylike" thing to do. This attitude was particularly pervasive in the 1930s, when many thousands of male workers had lost their jobs due to the stock market crash and the collapse of the banking industry.

After the military surrenders, after the wars that testosterone and megalomania had started were over, these gals were unceremoniously told to head home. *(Thank you, but your services are no longer required. Don't let the door hit you in the tuchas on your way out!)*

Racism also escalated in new and toxic ways during wartime. While anti-German sentiment was rampant in America during World War I, it paled in comparison to the "patriotic" stateside actions of World War II. For example, the Japanese-American families who were imprisoned in concentration camps on the West Coast during the 1940s lost not only their freedom, but their homes, businesses, personal possessions and financial assets. Poof, gone! Just like that. African-American and Mexican-American women who had the opportunity to earn decent wages for the first time in their lives during World War II, were quickly demoted to their low-income, dead-end jobs after V-E Day.

The lesson is this: American women always cleaned up the mess. They rolled up their sleeves to tackle the problem — whether it was war or economic catastrophe — while it was happening. They nursed the sick and the injured, both at home and on the battlefield. They waited for those they loved to return and mourned when they didn't come back at all.

Right:
Snapshot, gravesite. Latina women and children, Tulare County, California, 1940s. (Below: enlarged portion of image at the right, showing boy in pilot's cap.)

In the end, it was the women who healed the country's terrible wounds, whether they were physical, emotional or spiritual.

You might ask yourself:
How did they manage? How did American women survive these types of overwhelming, life-altering problems and challenges?

This Page:
Left: Snapshot, inscribed on back "Missing Him; December 5, 1942."

Top: Photobooth image, inscribed "Friends at Camp Knight; Buddy & Lucille," 1940s.

Bottom: Snapshot, woman wearing an army jacket and holding a beer, 1940s.

They depended on

each other.

Marguerite

Chapter 11: Now, It's Your Turn!

"The only person I really believe in is me."

—Debbie Harry (1945-), American songwriter, actress and lead singer of the band Blondie

If you have a memory like a steel trap, it's possible that you recall what I was talking about in the beginning of this book. You and your fellow females are actually on an action-packed Heroine's Journey, all day, every day. And guess what? Just like Dorothy realized at the end of "The Wizard of Oz," women have always had the power to go where they want to go.

The question is, where the heck are we going? Are we taking that "Road to Nowhere" you always hear so much about? Who's driving? Should I bring a sweater? What's the sleeping situation going to be like? Will I have an extra pillow if I want one? I don't sleep well on flat, prison-style pillows ...

Slow your roll, sister! You don't need all the answers right this very second. Actually, you might be unclear on what the questions are, and that's perfectly fine. Most of the time, stumbling around in the dark is the only way to find the light switch.

The impact of all this "Thanks to Her" photo flipping and historical yammering might not even hit you for a few days, or a month, or a year. But, mark my words: Someday, it will all be clear to you.

What will happen then? Well, you will probably notice a teeny-tiny grain of cautious enthusiasm or persistent curiosity poke, poke, poking you right in your psyche. Your photo-inspired epiphany might even manifest as a general sense of pissed-offedness. Maybe you'll wake up one morning with an unexplainable yet overwhelming sense of righteous indignation. (One time, this happened to me and I got so mad, I threw a fully wrapped Egg McMuffin out my car window while I was driving in rush-hour traffic. I really hadn't solved my problem with this gesture, because I was starving and late for work. It also wasn't great for the environment, but it was kinda over-the-top dramatic, and I have to admit, I felt a little better.)

Anyway, as I was saying, if you're irritable about the state of your female existence, that's OK! Take that feeling and run with it! Keep that teeny-tiny grain of anger alive, because it's going to fuel your motivation.

That's what our foremothers did in times of war, in times of economic desperation, in times of soul-crushing discrimination. These ladies did not have a road map to follow; they literally made solutions up

This Page:
Top: Snapshot, Two women staring into a crystal ball, late 1940s. The future was not always clear, but early 20th century American women were able to roll with the changes, no matter what obstacles came their way.

Bottom: Snapshot, girl walking alone, labeled "Birmingham, 1952." By the mid-century mark, American females had learned that the road less taken can often be the very best way to go!

Opposite Page:
Photobooth images, 1930s to 1950s. Different eras, different ladies. Same smile that says: "Yes, I can, and so can you."

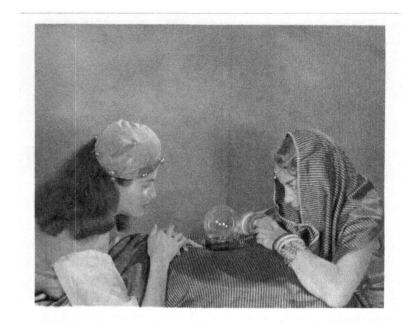

Previous Spread, Left
Top Left: Outdoor portrait, Marguerite posing on a burro at Happy Hollow, a picture studio and amusement park in Hot Springs, Arkansas, late 1900s or early 1910s.

Top Right: Snapshot, dancer performing in a peacock feather costume, 1940s.

Bottom Left: Snapshot, young lady in a white gown with a bouquet of roses, late 1940s.

Bottom Right: Snapshot, lady wearing a man's hat and smoking a skull-head pipe, 1940s.

Previous Spread, Right
Snapshot, female musicians Meta, Lillian and Hazel, late 1940s or early 1950s.

as they went along. They relied on something deep inside themselves, in their spirits, to guide them. Call it an internal compass or X-chromosome intuition or the ovarian superpower — it all had the same effect. In many instances, it was unconventional thinking, fueled by feminine instinct, that helped entire families survive.

Whenever life gets you down and you feel truly miserable, remember that you come from strong female stock. It doesn't matter whether you can trace your ancestry back to the Mayflower or whether your family has quietly disappeared into the black hole of the Witness Protection Program. (These things happen.) Just know that at some time in your past, women were taking care of business and working their big magic, and you have benefited from all their efforts.

Maybe you, like Dorothy, were never told you had intelligence and power. You had to discover that all by yourself, without the assistance of a scarecrow, a lion, and a silver dude in a tinfoil suit. I can only hope that you had red, sparkly shoes at your disposal during this process.

Family photographs can help us realize that our talents, goals and dreams were planted like beautiful, gorgeous seeds by those incredible women who lived before us. These messages, their wonderful legacies, were never lost. We just had to pause, reflect, and find them for ourselves.

I hope you are ready to pull your family photos out of the dark boxes and bins where they are stored and let the flowers of inspiration bloom. As you go forward on your merry way, please remember those ladies. Without their accomplishments and activism, we would not enjoy access to higher education, the right to vote, or the ability to use birth control. Yes, thanks to them, your uterus does not have to dictate your destiny. Ain't it great?

```
As women, we have the power to create a
societal shift. We also hold the keys to
our Queendoms. Check your closets, attics,
basements and storage rooms. You may find
them in a long-neglected shoebox full of
family photos. Love them. Share them.
Live with them in mind.
```

Women's History Resources

The Library of Congress

On this spread, and throughout this book, you will find a variety of free-use images that the Library of Congress has graciously loaned to this author for inclusion in "Thanks to Her." Actually, the fact that they are free use, means they are available to anyone, so I'm not special or anything like that. The library's photography collection is a truly amazing resource for anyone who wants to learn more about American history and it's just waiting for you! Visit the Library of Congress at: www.loc.gov.

Thanks to the Fashionistas

One of the most challenging aspects of working on "Thanks to Her" involved dating the individual photographs. Often, fashion is a key indicator of time, place and the subject's lifestyle. Since I am humbled by the genius of women like Coco Chanel and Diana Vreeland, I know better than to mess with the facts when it comes to all things fashion-related. When I needed help in this area, I turned to these resources:

Vintage Dancer

Debbie Sessions, the owner of the website Vintage Dancer, is actually the person who was able to identify the clothing that Hazel (the cover girl of this book) was wearing. For this, I am eternally grateful. Debbie specializes in helping people connect to vintage clothing via a motherlode of online resources. In curating her shop pages, Debbie conducts extensive historical research. She is your go-to gal for costumes or a personal vintage-inspired wardrobe that reflects any time period from the Victorian Era to the 1960s. Visit her online and read her awesome blog at: www.VintageDancer.com.

"The Ultimate Fashion History Channel" on YouTube

Professor Amanda Hallay (LIM College in New York) is a teacher, author, fashion historian and presenter who specializes in the relationship between culture and clothing. Her lectures can be enjoyed via "The Ultimate Fashion History," the incredible, fact-filled YouTube channel that she created and hosts. I can't say enough about Amanda's brilliance and her extremely engaging presentation style. Visit her online at: www.AmandaHallay.com.

Above:
Elizabeth Cady Stanton, seated, and Susan B. Anthony, standing, three-quarter length portrait. [Between 1880-1902] [Photograph] https://www.loc.gov/item/97500087.

Opposite Page:
Top Left: Heyn Photo, photographer. Stella Yellow Shirt and baby , ca. 1899. [Photograph] https://www.loc.gov/item/92508778/.

Top Right: Mary Church Terrell, portrait, seated, facing front, None. [Between 1880-1900, printed later] Photograph. https://www.loc.gov/item/97500102/.

Bottom Left: Lange, D., photographer. Destitute pea pickers in California. Mother of seven children. Age thirty-two. San Luis Obispo County, Nipomo, California, United States, March 1936. [Photograph] https://www.loc.gov/item/2017762891/.

Bottom Right: Miss Sarah Anderson, a Washington suffragist, enjoys a "puff" at the Chevy Chase Country Club, 1920. https://www.loc.gov/pictures/item/2016827565/

Hey! What Happened After That?

The timeline of "Thanks to Her" pauses in 1950 for several reasons. First of all, I thought it was an appropriate place for a "commercial break" — as they used to say on network TV back in the day. Secondly, the mid-century mark represented a shift in the nation's priorities. Weary after decades of economic struggle and war, Americans headed home in the early 1950s to cocoon, find some kind of new normalcy, and dream up a better future.

    In terms of women's history, this transition coincided with the debut of writer and philosopher Simone de Beauvoir's landmark book, "The Second Sex." Originally published in French in 1949 as "Le Deuxième Sexe," de Beauvoir's work provided a scathing analysis of the patriarchy and its process of defining women's lives only in terms of their relationships to men. By stating that, "One is not born, but becomes a woman," she crystallized the concept of sex-gender distinction and laid the groundwork for modern feminist thought.

    Regardless of their educational achievements, mid-century women were valued for their physical appearance and their connections to hearth and home. They might have had robust intellects and revolutionary ideas, but they were discouraged from sharing them. As a result, many women were forced to lead stifled, fragmented lives. Or, as de Beauvoir succinctly put it, "Her wings are cut and then she is blamed for not knowing how to fly." Sound familiar? Good golly, it's deja-flippin'-vu all over again!

    Unfortunately, many of the issues de Beauvoir examined decades ago are alive and well today. Far from being a quaint remnant of a distant and less enlightened time, "The Second Sex" remains valid, powerful and eerily prescient. In fact, it's the literary equivalent of an episode of "The Twilight Zone." So, here we are. Let's not say goodbye to the idea of "Thanks to Her" with the dawn of the 1950s. Let's just say we'll pick things up where we left off the next time we meet ...

Thanks to Them

Couldn't Have Done It Without You!

In the interest of giving credit where credit is due, I am sharing this bibliography. I hope that these authors inspire you as they did me. Their collective genius made my research and this book possible. I also want to give a shout out to Blanca Datro at the Chicago Public Library. She not only offered her unfailingly cheerful assistance throughout this project, she taught me how to get potholes fixed with the City of Chicago's 311 app. *Gotta love that!*

Allen, Frederick Lewis.
Only Yesterday: An Informal History of the 1920s. New York, Perennial Classics, 2000.

Allen, Frederick Lewis.
Since Yesterday: The 1930s in America, September 3, 1929 - September 3, 1939. New York, Perennial Library, 1986.

Beauvoir, Simone de.
The Second Sex. New York : Alfred A. Knopf, 2010.

Blum, Stella.
Everyday Fashions of the Thirties as Pictured in Sears Catalogs. New York: Dover Publications, 1986.

Blum, Stella.
Everyday Fashions of the Twenties as Pictured in Sears and Other Catalogs. New York: Dover Publications, 1981.

Calasibetta, Charlotte Mankey.
The Fairchild Dictionary of Fashion. New York, Fairchild Publications, 2003.

Coffin, Sarah.
The Jazz Age: American Style in the 1920s. Cleveland, Ohio, The Cleveland Museum of Art, 2017.

Cullen-DuPont, Kathryn.
Encyclopedia of Women's History in America. New York, Facts on File, Inc., 2000.

Cummins, D. Dwayne.
Contrasting Decades, the 1920s and 1930s. Encino, Calif., Glencoe Publishing Co., 1980.

Cunningham, Patricia A.
Reforming Women's Fashion, 1850-1920: Politics, Health and Art. Kent, Ohio, The Kent State University Press, 2003.

Dumenil, Lynn.
American Women and World War I. Chapel Hill, The University of North Carolina Press, 2017.

Eichler, Lillian.
The New Book of Etiquette. New York, Garden City Publishing Company, Inc., 1939

Gavin, Lettie.
American Women in World War I: They Also Served. Boulder, University Press of Colorado, 1997.

Gilbert, George.
Photography: The Early Years. New York, Harper & Row Publishers, 1980.

Goranin, Nakki.
American Photobooth. New York, W.W. Norton & Company, 2008.

Hartmann, Susan M.
The Home Front and Beyond: American Women in the 1940s. Boston: Twayne Publishers, 1982.

Hirsch, Julia.
Family Photographs: Content, Meaning, and Effect. New York, Oxford University Press, 1981.

Howard, Vicki.
From Main Street to the Mall: The Rise and Fall of the American Department Store. Philadelphia, University of Pennsylvania Press, 2015.

King, Charles R.
Children's Health in America: A History. New York: Twayne Publishers; Maxwell Macmillan International, 1993.

Kirkham, Pat, editor.
Women Designers in the USA, 1900-2000: Diversity and Difference. New Haven, Yale University Press, 2000.

Lunardi, Christine, Ph.D.
What Every American Should Know About Women's History. Holbrook, Mass., Bob Adams, Inc., 1994.

Macdonald, Anne L.
Feminine Ingenuity: Women and Invention in America. New York, Ballantine Books, 1992.

Marcus, Alan I.
Technology in America: A Brief History. Fort Worth, Harcourt Brace College Publishers, 1999.

Motz, Marilyn Ferris and Browne, Pat, editors.
Making the American Home: Middle-Class Women and Domestic Material Culture, 1840-1940. Bowling Green, Ohio: Bowling Green State University Popular Press, 1988.

National Cloak & Suit Co.
Women's Fashions of the Early 1900s: An Unabridged Republication of "New York Fashions, 1909." New York: Dover Publications, 1992.

Neth, Mary.
Preserving the Family Farm: Women, Community and the Foundations of Agribusiness in the Midwest, 1900-1940. Baltimore: Johns Hopkins University Press, 1995.

Olian, JoAnne, editor.
Everyday Fashions, 1909-1920, as Pictured in Sears Catalogs. New York, Dover, 1995.

Olian, JoAnne.
Everyday Fashions of the Fifties as Pictured in Sears Catalogs. Mineola, N.Y.: Dover Publications, 2002.

Olian, JoAnne.
Everyday Fashions of the Forties as Pictured in Sears Catalogs. New York: Dover Publications, 1992.

Parkin, Katherine J.
Women at the Wheel: A Century of Buying, Driving and Fixing Cars. Philadelphia: University of Pennsylvania Press, 2017.

Pellicer, Raynal.
Photobooth: The Art of the Automatic Portrait. New York, Abrams, 2010.

Perry, Dame & Co.
Women and Children's Fashions of 1917. New York: Dover Publications, 1992.

Phillips, Tom.
The Postcard Century: 2000 Cards and Their Messages. New York, Thames & Hudson, 2000.

Scharff, Virginia.
Taking the Wheel: Women and the Coming of the Motor Age. New York: Free Press; Toronto: Collier Macmillan Canada: Maxwell Macmillan International, 1991.

Schneider, Dorothy and Carl J.
American Women in the Progressive Era, 1900-1920. New York, Anchor Books, Doubleday, 1993.

Shubert, Betty Kriesel.
Out-of-Style: A Modern Perspective of How, Why and When Vintage Fashions Evolved. Mission Viejo, Calif.: Flashback Publishing, 2013.

Simons, Margaret A.
Beauvoir and The Second Sex: Feminism, Race, and the Origins of Existentialism. Lanham, Md.: Rowman & Littlefield Publishers, 1999.

Snyder-Haug, Diane.
Antique & Vintage Clothing: A Guide to Dating & Valuation of Women's Clothing 1850-1940. Paducah, Ky.: Collector Books, 1997.

Strasser, Susan.
Never Done: A History of American Housework. New York: Pantheon Books, 1982.

Steinem, Gloria.
Outrageous Acts and Everyday Rebellions. New York: Holt, Rinehart and Winston, 1983.

Steinem, Gloria.
Revolution from Within: A Book of Self-Esteem. Boston: Little, Brown and Company, 1992.

Taylor, Maureen Alice.
Family Photo Detective: Learn How to Find Genealogy Clues in Old Photos and Solve Family Photo Mysteries. Cincinnati, Ohio, Family Tree Books, 2013.

Vare, Ethlie Ann.
Mothers of Invention: From the Bra to the Bomb: Forgotten Women & Their Unforgettable Ideas. New York, Quill, 1989.

Vaule, Rosamond B.
As We Were: American Photographic Postcards, 1905-1930. Boston, David R. Godine, Publisher, 2004.

Youcha, Geraldine.
Minding the Children: Child Care in America from Colonial Times to the Present. New York: Scribner, 1995.

Zeitz, Joshua.
Flapper: A Madcap Story of Sex, Style, Celebrity, and the Women Who Made America Modern. New York, Crown Publishers, 2006.

Ziegelman, Jane and Coe, Andrew.
A Square Meal: A Culinary History of the Great Depression. New York, NY: Harper, an Imprint of Harper Collins Publishers, 2016.

Thanks to You, Too!

It would have been impossible for me to have imagined or produced this book without the assistance of a number of awesome women. From the visual realm, I have to thank Lisa Maraldi of Maraldi Design, who was always there to lend her expertise, and Connie Ricca, my college buddy and fellow photojournalist, who is eternally optimistic. I am also grateful to my spiritual cheerleaders, Annie Hayashi and Mary Krebs Smyth. In recent months, my sister, sister-in-laws, cousins, nieces and assorted female relations have been kind enough to indulge me as I described this book and its direction. Most of the time, they even stayed awake! Above all, I thank my daughter Flynn, for being funny, creative and fiercely determined — and for just being. And THANK YOU for reading!

Made in the USA
Monee, IL
21 December 2021